You Made My Day

FOUR GENERATIONS OF KOSHER COOKING

by Evelyn Gold

Robert Davies Publishing

MONTREAL—TORONTO—PARIS

You Made My Day

You Made My Day

The title of this book came to mind while talking to my cousin, Marlene Briskin. Marlene's late mother, Leah, and my mother were first cousins but were actually more like sisters. During our conversations, Marlene would remind me how frequently Ma used to say, "You Made My Day" - usually in response to a compliment on her wardrobe, a new hair style, or a special meal she had prepared. Of course, nothing made her day more than a phone call from one of her grandchildren. As you read through this book, I hope it makes your day too!

My mother, Chana Schiff Katz

Dedication

In 1952 my sister Clara, married Murray Silver. In 1960, I married Phil Gold. Between the four of us we had six children. My mother made sure to tell anyone and everyone that her children were "silver" and "gold" but her grandchildren were the "diamonds".

This book is dedicated to my mother and to her "diamonds": Elaine, Howard and Steven Silver; Ian, Josie and Joel Gold; and to their spouses and children.

Our family tree, 1992

Acknowledgments

There are many people whom I would like to thank for making this book possible. In particular, I would like to thank Estella 'Stella' Bajoyo – the link between my mother's kitchen and mine. As my mother grew older and needed assistance with everyday tasks, Estella would spend a few days a week with her. It was during this time that Estella first tried many recipes with my mother. They got along well and Ma jokingly referred to herself as "Stella's Supervisor" while Stella would call my mother "Fancy Lady". Together they cooked, wrote recipes and, in particular, had many philosophical discussions. This union eventually led to a wonderful friendship, despite their age difference. This book could not have been written without Stella, who helped me painstakingly recreate and test each recipe, and also provided me with many anecdotes quoted from my mother.

I am grateful to my sister, Clara, who during the writing of this book made me laugh until my sides ached,[1] as we reminisced about our childhood. We talked about the afternoon Hebrew school we attended and our friends, including those our mother liked and those she did not.[2] We also discussed our favourite foods, diets, and our extended families. Although many of these experiences were not necessarily all that humorous when they occurred, they seem so now. I feel that our melded pasts serve as the solid foundation for the sisterly bond we are so fortunate to share.[3]

I am indebted to my family and friends who took the time to find many recipes that had never before been recorded and to the people who reminded me of many stories retold in this book. The credits for these recipes and anecdotes go to Stella, Marlene Briskin, Sylvia Feder,

---

[1] Whenever Clara and I laughed, without Ma being aware of what we were laughing about, she would always remark, "Nu, as long as you're laughing, I'm happy!"

[2] *Schlechteh Chaverim firen avec fun veyg* (Bad friends lead you off the straight and narrow).

[3] Whenever my mother spoke to Clara or me she usually asked, "Did you speak to Chavah today?" or "Did you speak to Clara today?". This was followed by, "So, what did SHE have to say?"

Riva Freedman, Sheila Kussner, Devra Rosenthall[4], Masha Schiff, Phyllis Schmeltzer, Schmiel Schreiber, Clara, Elaine, Howard, Steven, Jennifer, Phil, Josie, Cleve, Ian and Joel.

I am grateful to Lianne Arbour and Anna Cuccovia for typing the original manuscript. Particular thanks to Lianne for listening to me repeat the same stories as I wrote each section of this book. The *pièce de résistance* was her coming to the rescue during my computer crisis.

My appreciation goes to Phil, Clara, Masha Schiff and to Michael Herschorn, for their translations, interpretations and transliterations of many Yiddish expressions, and for placing them into proper figurative context.

I am most grateful to Ellen Lechter-Green for her skill, competence and professionalism in proofing and editing. In essence *You Made My Day* has maintained its flavour which is essential to a cookbook of this kind.

Thanks to Joe Donahue for his superb photography.

Special thanks to my children, who have always been kind, caring and supportive in my endeavours. Needless to say, they outdid themselves when I undertook this project. I credit their high standards and creativity for helping me transform this cookbook into one worthy of space in any *balabostah's* [5] kitchen.

To you Joel, I genuinely appreciated your honesty when tasting almost everything we prepared. I remember one occasion when I actually heard you say, "I don't remember Bubby making *all* this fabulous food!" In fact, many of these recipes were made long before you were born.

To you Ian, thanks for always reading my revisions on demand, nearly every time you spent an all-too-brief weekend in Montreal. Your comments, always delivered with sensitivity and tact, served as my impetus to continue with this work.

---

[4] Whenever Ma met Devra at the bank, she told her that Phil would one day win the "Noble Prize". Actually she meant the "Nobel Prize".

[5] Excellent homemaker and cook

My mother and Cleve comparing recipes in the country.

My mother and Stella in the kitchen.

To you Cleve, thanks for getting some of my mother's recipes and comments on tape while vacationing at *It-L-Do*. You made my mother laugh and you made her very happy. I feel fortunate to have been there on that afternoon in July.

To you Josie, there are no words with which I can adequately thank you for the design and layout of this book. You have tremendous talent; a talent which seems to come so naturally, yet I know how many hours were spent with every page. You had to deal with my cut and paste pages yet you always managed to turn out great results and I could not have completed this book without you. As Bubby would have said: *"Joselah, mein kindt, you have a puhr goldeneh hendt!"* ("Josie, my child, you have a pair of golden hands!") and, "I speak the truth". I feel that I too, have spoken the truth which comes from my heart.

Thank you, Phil, for the faith and confidence you've shown me from the onset of this project. To illustrate your input, one incident in particular comes to mind. When I mentioned that I would like to write a cookbook of my mother's recipes, your eyes lit up! You spent the next day totally involved in trying to find the appropriate publisher. Your enthusiasm has always been overwhelming; hence *You Made My Day* was a *fait accompli* even before it was written. Actually, I felt that I had already missed the deadline for some unknown publisher. Therefore, I had to do my utmost [6] (outmost) in setting up a new deadline – a real one! You have my heartfelt thanks for your energetic excitement and for your love of creativity which has always been a wonderful model for <u>my</u> love of creativity. Your contagious sense of wonder made me wonder as to what would ultimately happen with *You Made My Day*. Your ongoing support in contrast to my ongoing uncertainties, proved to be the catalyst for the inspiration that I needed to start, continue and complete this work. The rest is history!

---

[6] My mother always used the word "outmost" instead of "utmost". Either way it makes sense!

Table of Contents

A family photograph sent to Mathilda in New York, Boryslav, circa 1920
Standing from left: Mother's brother Lipa, his wife Genia, my mother,
Mother's brothers Meilach and Usher
Seated from left: Mother's sister Pesel, my grandmother Sarah Schiff,
my grandfather Yitzchak Hertzfeld, Mother's brother Willie

Introduction

My mother, Chana Schiff, was born at home on May 26, 1907, in Boryslav, Poland, located at the foot of the Carpathian Mountains. She died in Montreal, Canada on January 21, 1993 in a hospital located at the foot of Mount Royal. She was the youngest of nine children - seven of whom survived past age ten. The entire family came to North America in the early 1920's.

The family lived in poverty, and my mother would sadly recall always feeling hungry except during the *Yom Tovim* (High Holidays). I can only surmise that when she arrived in Canada - the land of plenty - she vowed to herself that her children would never "go hungry" whatever the circumstances.

My mother's formal education was rather limited. Because she had to help support the family, she learned to sew and worked for many years in the "sweat shops" of Montreal's garment trade.

In retrospect, it seems ironic that she attended night school to learn English at an institution she referred to as "St. Georges", but it was actually Sir George Williams College (now Concordia University).

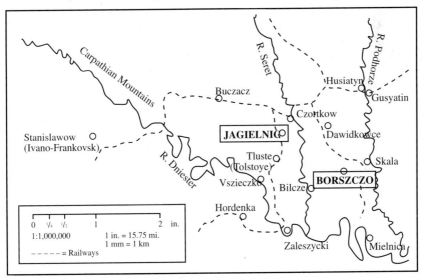

My mother's home town Boryslav (Borszcow), and my father's home town,
Jagdnitza (Jagielnic), now part of the Ukraine.

Although she never received a university education, Ma managed to develop her own philosophy about life and people and their diversities. Some of the maxims and proverbs that are incorporated in this book are based on the ideas she developed in her youth that served her well in many instances. I refer to them as her "words of wisdom". She would loosely translate them into English although they were usually best expressed in Yiddish - her *mama loshen* (mother tongue). My mother had her own version for many of these metaphors and I have done my best to translate them accurately in the figurative sense.

Do You Have a Minute?

Often when my mother telephoned, she began by asking me, "do you have a minute?" and continued by saying *"Got zol mir helfin dos vos ich ken nit arois zogen"* ("As G-d is my witness, allow Him to help me to deal with the issues that I have difficulty discussing with strangers") or *"Vas veniger redden altz gezunter"* ("the less said the better") and then "I have a lot to say, but I better not talk".

I hadn't responded to her first question and she hadn't taken a breath yet. Within the next few seconds she would repeat the question again, "do you have a minute?" This time it was different though, because she immediately began to confide her tale of woe to me. She described in great detail and with vigour the very same issues that she had planned to share with me at the outset of our conversation. These current problems were obviously of major concern. She always had a lot to say!

When I embarked on this project, my greatest fear was that I would not be able to convey my thoughts as easily as she was able to convey her stories. This was definitely not the case... Do you have a minute?

Just a Mother

When my sister, Clara, and I were growing up, Ma was "just a mother". This meant that she didn't have a job outside of the home. Today, she might be called a homemaker, housewife, or even a domestic engineer with a major in "Budget Balancing 101". I like to refer to her role as "Motherhood, Full Time".

Back then, only the upper class owned refrigerators. We had an ice box and Ma had to shop and prepare meals daily - which was, in itself, a full-time job. I vividly remember my parents purchasing their first "Frigidaire". The new fridge changed Ma's life - it gave her the opportunity to create new *petravahs* (delicacies or goodies).

While preparing this cookbook, I had to recall some of the delicacies of my childhood as well as the anecdotes that accompanied these *maichles* (yet another word for delicacies or goodies). It was only then that I realized I had never felt the pangs of hunger my mother frequently described. In fact, I only remember feeling stuffed as my mother fed me on demand (mostly hers) until I was old enough to do something about it.

My mother always wanted to be productive, and indeed she was. She was constantly seeking to learn, to accomplish, and to contribute more. Ma was a super homemaker because she loved to create. The presentation of a meal was as important to her as its taste.

My father was a man of few words and whenever Ma made something new or different, she sought his feedback to gain her confidence. After most meals, she would ask my father, "how did you enjoy it?" and he would invariably answer, "I was hungry, so I ate". But for Ma, that was praise enough.

I recall many occasions when my mother would clip recipes from *The Montreal Star, The Gazette* and *The Canadian Jewish News*. She would try them and usually comment afterwards, "it was much better after I fixed it up a little".

Ma loved having family and friends over. Even after my sister and I married, we continued to have dinner at my parents' home on Shabbat and holidays. After dinner we would return to our homes with care packages. When we had our own children, the care packages grew with the variety of dishes prepared to suit each and everyone's palate. Frequently, my mother offered to cook and bring the meals to our homes. Later, when it became difficult for her to carry heavy packages, she simply stated that she would have to cancel her delivery service. Of course, this meant that we were to pick up the *goodies* the moment they were ready. However, if we failed to do so, the food was sent to our homes via taxi.

Ma's care packages did more than provide us with home-cooked meals - they also ensured her ongoing involvement in our lives. Part of her daily routine was speaking with all members of the family to find out who was eating what and with whom.

Ma took great pleasure in serving us, even at an event or celebration. She would say, "Can I make you a plate?" and Phil would always respond, "Zap, I'm a plate". This teasing from either of her sons-in-law was always welcomed.

Phil and my mother at Phil's graduation from medical school, 1961
"Can I make you a plate?"

Place your Orders

Whenever I entertained, or even planned to entertain, I always received a telephone call that went something like this: "So when do you plan to start preparing? Can I do something for you? What would you like? Give me your order, I'm looking for business." After this preamble, she would finally ask, "hello, how are you?" After we discussed the other important issues no one said good-bye, we merely said "okay" and hung up the telephone. These conversations became the staples of our relationship. We would begin by discussing food until the topic led to other matters. Of course, our conversations also served a more basic purpose. I appreciated the advice and help, while Ma enjoyed giving it. I know she was especially flattered when I would tell her, "Whatever you're making, I'll be more than happy to serve!"

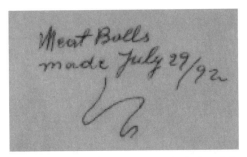

The cover of a typical package – labeled and dated.

Ma's enthusiasm and *joie de vivre* regarding food preparation and presentation equalled that of any professional. Just as she excelled in the kitchen she was also skilled with needle and thread. She loved to sew and took great pride in making cross-stitched tablecloths and place mats for both my sister and me. She also loved to make them for her grand-children or for friends who showed interest in her work.

In the last three years of her life she made many tablecloths, especially for Elaine, Ian and Josie. I encouraged her to sign them and naturally, she was delighted to do so. Josie was responsible for drawing her name in a cross-stitch pattern on each of the cloths. These tablecloths are precious to us as they are part of my mothers' legacy. We use them on Shabbat, holidays and other special occasions.

My mother sewing one of her famous tablecloths.

The finishing touch.

The Beginning of a Cookbook

The idea of a cookbook began about ten years ago. My husband Phil, thought it would be a way for Ma to feel she was still contributing to her family, but Ma was ambivalent. On one hand, she felt overwhelmed, but on the other hand, she felt flattered that Phil had so much respect for her accomplishments. However, since Ma had lost some of her eyesight and hearing by then, she couldn't undertake such a large task on her own. Because she couldn't complete this project herself, I felt a particular need to fulfill this dream by seeing this manuscript to fruition.

Ma never wrote anything down. She preferred to pass on her recipes by grabbing your hand and poking you in the shoulder to gain your undivided attention. Many of my friends left my house with sore shoulders after talking with my mother for a few hours, but they also left with more than a few suggestions on how to run their lives, their homes and their families.

The other reason for compiling this book is purely a selfish one. I wanted to try to recapture some of the personal exchanges between my mother and many members of the family. The expressions and one-liners have been reiterated over and over by *our group* and I wanted to preserve them in print.

This book has been a labour of love. It serves as a link with the past, and has given me much comfort in the present. I hope it will also provide a bridge for future generations of our family unit.

In closing I wish you *bonne chance* and hope you will enjoy your journey through this cookbook. I will consider this book a success if you experience even a fraction of the pleasure, joy and excitement that my mother did when she prepared these meals. However, should any of these recipes fail, do not despair; just remember: "It's not only the food, it's the company!"

Bon Appétit!
Evelyn Gold

"It's not only the food, it's the company!"

Me, my father, my mother and Clara, Prefontaine, 1943.

Ode to my Mother

'Ma' was a giving and loving mother,
We were two sisters who wanted a brother
However, that dream never came to pass
And so we had to make do – Alas!

Mother had talent – how she'd sew and cook,
Her cooking was special – no matter what it took.
She nurtured us with loving care,
and whatever she did, she was always fair!
(except when she forced me to eat!)

She was strict in her ways – with friends and with school,
I guess in those days, it was easy to rule.
Today, it's quite a different story,
And different times bring different glory.

At this time, I feel I'd like to state,
Just how much I do appreciate.
My sisters' work for all to see,
Her drive made this book a reality.

It was my job to encourage the writing of this book,
And I'm very excited when I look
at the recipes and anecdotes, there's nothing to hide,
It's a legacy given with a great deal of pride!

My "Yiddishe Mama" – I miss her so much,
A Classy Lady with a classy touch!
If she were to see this book, I know she'd say,
"Oh my G-d, *you made my day!*"

Clara Silver

Keeping Kosher

Kashruth: Preparation of food in accordance with Jewish dietary laws (the strict separation of dairy and meat or meat-derived foods).

Dairy:
Foods containing milk products only.

Meat:
Foods containing meat products only.

Parve:
Food products containing neither milk nor meat. Parve foods include everything that grows from the soil i.e. fruit, vegetables, nuts, coffee, spices, sugar; and salt, fish with fins and scales, and eggs.

Parve foods cooked in meat pots must be served as meat dishes. Likewise, parve foods cooked in dairy pots must be served as dairy dishes.

When I was growing up, Kashruth was observed in our home. It was never a problem for us; if anything, it made life more interesting. Mealtime, its preparation, and the variety of dishes, changed every day and therefore played a major role in our daily lives. Thus, the dining room table became the focal point for most of our conversations. Even though my parents frequently spoke to each other in Yiddish or Polish so that neither Clara nor I would understand, we were accustomed to hearing these languages and often would pick up the gist of the discussion. For example: In Yiddish we often heard *gornisht iz nisht shver, men darf nor kenen* (nothing is too difficult if we know how to do it). In Polish it was - *Vannah Ladnah?* (Isn't she pretty?)

When I got married and had children of my own, keeping a kosher kitchen was a tradition I wanted to continue. As Clara's extended family and my extended family have grown, we have spent week-ends together at our joint country home *It-L-Do*. Naturally, this means that there have been any number of cooks in the kitchen at any given time.

A few years ago, in order to avoid any confusion concerning the appropriate placement of dairy and meat utensils, I decided to label the various drawers and cupboards. The symbols I used were "M" for meat and "M" for milk (this should have been a "D" for dairy).

As I anxiously awaited everyone's reaction to my kosher codes, I suddenly realized that the joke was on me! No one noticed or even bothered to look at my blunder. Instead they placed the appropriate dishes in their proper places. Maintaining a kosher kitchen presented no problem after all!

Chalah

Chopped Liver

Eggplant

Halishkes

Sweet 'n' Sour Meatballs

Chicken Soup

Knaidlach

Roast Chicken

Breaded Zucchini

Carrot, Pineapple, Mandarin Orange Mishmash

Mushroom Patties

Onion Knishes

Potato Knishes

Potato Kugel

Varenekes

Vegetable Fried Rice

Baked Apples

Cookies

Shabbat

Holiday Treats

Light Lunches and Pastas

Salads, Sauces and Soups

Vegetables

Fish

Poultry

Meats

Desserts

Odds 'n' Ends

*Family life centres around the home and **Shabbat** is a fundamental part of Jewish tradition. Shabbat is certainly one of the most important and meaningful times of the week. For most families, it is when loved ones get together, be it in Synagogue or at home. This tradition continues to strengthen strong family ties for most Jews, even when some of the religious customs are no longer observed.*

***Shabbat** gatherings often help open the lines of communication between loved ones for this one evening a week. Whether you are young, old, single or married, when you sit around the **Shabbat** table you cannot help but remember that you belong to a family. Inevitably, the bonds that unite us with our past and with each other, are solidified. It is not surprising that families who meet and celebrate together often instill in their children a greater sense of security and self-worth.*

One of my mother's handmade chalah covers

Chalah
serves 10 - 12

Ingredients
1 Tbsp. yeast
2 eggs
2 tsp. sugar
2 Tbsp. oil
1 1/4 cups lukewarm water
4 1/2 cups flour (sifted)
2 tsp. salt
1 egg yolk
4 Tbsp. poppy seeds

Directions
This recipe should be prepared in a warm area.

Combine yeast with 1/4 cup of lukewarm water, add sugar, let stand until foamy. Sift flour and salt into bowl. Make a well in the centre of the mixture and drop in the eggs, oil and remaining water.

Knead dough on a floured surface until smooth and elastic. Place in a lightly oiled bowl, cover with a towel and let rise until it doubles in size (approximately 1 hour). Keep in warm area. When it doubles in size punch down and wait until it rises again to double its size in bulk (approximately 15 minutes). Punch down again.

Divide into three strips and braid. Cover with towel and allow to rise, approximately 20 minutes more. Brush with egg yolk and sprinkle with poppy seeds.

Bake at 375° for 50 minutes, or until brown.

Chopped Liver
serves 4 - 6

Ingredients
1 lb. chicken livers (lightly broiled)
2 hard boiled eggs
1 tsp. garlic powder
3 large onions (chopped)
1/4 cup water
1/4 tsp. sugar or sugar substitute
1/2 cup oil
☞ approx. 9" fry pan

Directions
Stew onions in water until all of the water is absorbed. Add the oil and livers to the onions. Sauté until onions are golden brown (approximately 12 - 15 minutes). Grind onion-liver mixture and eggs in meat grinder. Add salt, pepper and sugar or sweetener, to taste.

Refrigerate before serving.

Esn geyt nit far kein tantz.
Eating comes before dancing.

Eggplant

serves 6 - 8

Ingredients
1 large eggplant
1 Tbsp. oil
1 Tbsp. lemon juice
dash of sugar
dash of salt

Directions
Puncture eggplant with a fork and place in a tightly sealed plastic bag. Microwave on high for 15 minutes. If the eggplant is not soft, continue for another 4 minutes.

Remove from bag while the eggplant is still hot. Wash with cold water immediately (this will make the skin removal easier). Chop, add salt, sugar, oil and lemon juice. Taste and adjust.

Add an additional touch of oil on top of eggplant when storing in a jar. If eggplant seeds are dark in colour (black), remove all seeds. Eggplant should look white in colour.

Ma used to broil the eggplant, whole, for $1/2$ hour until the skin was seared and black. Stella introduced my mother to the microwave oven, and she approved mainly because the eggplant took less time to make, the colour remained white and the kitchen did not smell of ashes for hours after the eggplant was cooked. Kudos to Stella!

Halishkes

cabbage rolls
makes 24 - 30

Ingredients
1 large cabbage
1 apple (sliced)
2 lbs. minced steak
1 tomato (sliced)
4 eggs
3 cups water
3/4 cup long grain rice (uncooked)
salt and pepper, to taste
2 Tbsp. brown sugar
2 tsp. soya sauce
1/2 cup ketchup
2 Tbsp. strong dry garlic spare-rib sauce
2 19 oz. cans tomato juice
2 Tbsp. honey
1/2 tsp. garlic powder
2 onions (sliced)
1/2 cup golden raisins
1/2 cup matzo meal
☛ approx. 20 quart pot

A gast oyf a vayle, zet far a mayle.
A guest for a while, sees for a mile.

Directions

Prepare meat as in Sweet 'n' Sour Meatballs (page 32) with one exception: use uncooked rice instead of matzo meal. Set aside.

Blanche cabbage, separate leaves and allow to cool.

To prepare halishkes, place 2 Tbsp. of meat mixture into each leaf at the hardest end. Roll from thick to thin and tuck leaves in – right side first and then left side.

Prepare sauce and layer alternately with the halishkes in the following order:
slices of cabbage, leftover from centre of the cabbage
onion
$1/4$ of the halishkes
apple slices
tomato slices
$1/4$ cup of the halishkes
$1/4$ cup ketchup
raisins
$1/4$ of the halishkes
brown sugar
19 oz. can tomato juice
$1/4$ of the halishkes

Add honey, water, 1 can of tomato juice and $1/4$ cup of ketchup. Bring to a boil. Lower flame, cover and simmer for 2 hours. Just before 2 hours of simmering, taste and adjust with salt and pepper.

Can be frozen. To reheat, defrost, place in pot and add a drop of water, ketchup, tomato juice and honey. Cover and reheat on medium flame for 10 - 15 minutes. Stir occasionally until hot. Halishkes taste better after having been frozen.

Delicious!

Sweet 'n' Sour Meatballs

with giblets (chicken fricassee) or without giblets
makes 36 meatballs

Meat ingredients

1 lb. minced steak

or

$1/2$ lb. minced veal + $1/2$ lb. minced steak (beef)

19 oz. can tomato juice

$1/2$ tsp. garlic powder

1 tsp. soya sauce

1 Tbsp. garlic spare-rib sauce (strong)

2 Tbsp. brown sugar

$1 1/4$ cups of ketchup

2 eggs

3 Tbsp. honey

$1/2$ cup matzo meal

3 onions (diced)

1 lb. giblets (optional)

Sauce ingredients

$1/4$ tsp. garlic powder

1 Tbsp. brown sugar

3 onions (diced)

$1/2$ cup ketchup

19 oz. can tomato juice

☛ approx. 20 quart pot

Directions

Add ¼ tsp. garlic powder, 1 Tbsp. brown sugar, ½ cup ketchup, soya sauce, garlic sauce, eggs, matzo meal to meat and set aside.

Mix sauce ingredients in the pot and bring to a boil. Lower flame but keep sauce boiling.

Wet hands when shaping meatballs so they will be smooth and not stick. Meatballs should be small (1" in diameter - bite size). Drop meatballs into boiling sauce. To stir, shake pot from side to side (pot should be moved quickly). Do not mix with a spoon or meatballs will fall apart.

When all meatballs have been formed and dropped into the sauce, add ¼ cup ketchup and 19 oz. tomato juice and 3 Tbsp. honey to the sauce.

Cover and let simmer for 1 hour on medium flame.

Can be frozen. To reheat, defrost and add a drop of water and a drop of ketchup. Place pot on stove on medium to low flame, uncovered, until hot. Do not mix. Stir by moving pot quickly from side to side.

Meatballs with giblets

Clean giblets with boiling water and add to sauce just before meatballs.

House guests are like fish, after three days they begin to smell.

Chicken Soup
serves 12 - 15

Ingredients
3$\frac{1}{2}$ lb. chicken (cut into eighths and skinned)
3 large carrots (peeled)
3 parsley roots (peeled)
1 large onion
2 celery stalks
$\frac{1}{2}$ medium-size green pepper (seeded)
1 tsp. sugar
salt, to taste
3 quarts water
1 turnip
2 scallions
☞ approx. 20 quart pot

Directions
Fill pot with water and chicken. Bring to a boil and skim off the foam, which is fat, as it comes to the top. Add vegetables and simmer for 30 minutes. Taste and adjust by adding salt and sugar.

Allow to cool and skim off the fat again.

The boiled chicken can be eaten or used for other recipes such as Southern Fried Chicken (page 147) or Chicken Salad (page 105).

Freeze soup without the vegetables. Chicken can be frozen separately as well.

The women of my mother's generation were taught that men had to be served at the table. In her day, marriage meant that each partner had a specific role and the woman's role was in the kitchen. Hence, when I got married, my mother assumed that the tradition of "women in the kitchen" would continue. However, much to her dismay, my husband loved to putter around the kitchen. This change was hard for my mother to accept.

On Shabbat, everyone usually ate together. There was always a variety of entrées, poultry, vegetables, etc. Frequently, when any one of us had meatballs, fish or chopped liver, we would pass on soup when it was being served but wait for the main course.

Ma respected and loved Phil but she wanted me to show him respect - at least, respect as she perceived it. Her way of guiding me was to poke me under the table and whisper loudly, "does Phil want soup?"

Phil would always respond by asking; "Ma, are you angry with me?" The conversation would end by her saying; "It's your wife's pleasure to serve you and it should continue for many, many years to come!"

I find myself saying the same thing to my daughter; "Josie, does Cleve want soup?"

Gelt vakst nit oyf di beimer.
Money doesn't grow on trees.

Knaidlach
(matzo balls)
makes 20

Ingredients
1 cup matzo meal
4 Tbsp. liquid chicken stock or water
2 tsp. salt
4 Tbsp. oil
4 eggs

Directions
Separate eggs, beat egg whites until stiff and set aside. Mix all other ingredients together and then fold gently into egg whites. Place in refrigerator for 15 minutes.

Wet hands with cold water to form mixture into balls 1" in diameter. Drop the balls into boiling chicken soup, lower flame but allow the soup to continue boiling. Allow matzo balls to cook for 20 - 25 minutes.

Cannot be frozen.

Men vil zich elterin ober men vil nit zayne alt.
Everyone wants to grow older but nobody wants to be old.

Roast Chicken

serves 6 - 8

Ingredients
5 lb. chicken
1 cup ketchup
1 cup honey
garlic powder, enough to lightly cover chicken
dry chicken stock, enough to lightly cover chicken
1 tsp. oil
1 large onion (sliced, optional)
☞ large roasting pan

Directions
Mix honey and ketchup together and set aside. Clean chicken with boiling water and season with mixture of dry garlic powder and dry chicken stock and then with mixture of ketchup and honey. Place the seasoned chicken in the roasting pan, covered with oil and onion.

Bake, uncovered, at 425° for 20 minutes.

Baste a few times. Lower temperature to 300° and cover. Continue to bake and baste for an additional 60 - 80 minutes. Check to see if it is soft.

Can be frozen.

Oyf nit geyn un nit foren zol men keyn kharote nit hoben.
Don't look back with regret.

Breaded Zucchini

makes 32 servings

Ingredients

4 zucchinis (each cut into 8 pieces)
3 eggs (beaten)
salt and pepper, to taste
garlic powder, to taste
1 cup matzo meal or breadcrumbs
☛ approx. 9" fry pan and cookie sheet

Directions

Wash, peel and cut zucchini into eighths. Mix dry ingredients together in a bowl and then bread the zucchini by dipping it into the mixture.

Beat eggs and dip breaded zucchini into the beaten eggs. Dip into dry mixture again and then into eggs for a final time.

Heat the oil in the fry pan. Fry zucchini for about 2 minutes on each side until golden brown. Place on paper towel to remove the excess oil. Cool. Reheat in hot oven on the cookie sheet prior to serving.

Best served fresh.

Reden iz silber un schveigen iz gold.
Talking is silver and silence is golden.

Carrot, Pineapple, Mandarin Orange Mishmash

serves 5

Ingredients

12 oz. can pineapple tidbits (with juice)
12 oz. can mandarin oranges (with juice)
2 packets sweetener or 2 Tbsp. sugar (optional)
salt, to taste
8 fresh carrots (peeled)
or
2 19 oz. cans cooked baby carrots (drained)

Directions

If carrots are fresh, cook until soft. Drain and slice into small pieces.
Add pineapple tidbits with juice and the mandarin oranges with juice.
Bring to a boil. Taste, and if necessary, add sweetener or sugar and salt.
Taste again and adjust.

If carrots are canned, drain and add to pineapple tidbits with juice and
mandarin oranges with juice. Bring mixture to a boil. Taste to determine
amount of sweetener. Adjust.

Note

Fresh carrots are usually better as they are much sweeter.

Easy, pretty and delicious!

Mushroom Patties
makes 4 dozen

Dough
1 lb. puff dough

Filling ingredients
1 1/2 lb. mushrooms
1 onion
2 small green peppers
1 small red peppers
5 carrots
1/2 turnip
3 parsley roots
1 Tbsp. salt
1/2 tsp. pepper
1 Tbsp. garlic powder
2 cups Special K cereal (crushed)
5 celery stalks
3 scallions
2 Tbsp. oil

☞ approx. 15 quart pot and 12 cup muffin tin with 1 1/2" bottom

---

A khasorn di kaleh, tsu shein.
The flaw is that things are too good.

Directions

Wash, grate* and stew vegetables in oil, covered, over medium flame, until tender (approximately 5 minutes). Uncover and cook for an additional 5 minutes. If not tender, continue to cook for an additional 2 - 3 minutes. Remove from flame. Add crushed Special K cereal, salt, pepper and garlic powder. Mix and set aside.

Roll dough on floured board until it's ⅛" in thickness. Use a glass to make circles out of the dough and place in the muffin tins.

Spoon vegetable mixture (about 1 Tbsp.) into muffin tin onto the dough. Patties should be about half full in the muffin tin.

Bake at 350° for 20 - 25 minutes, or until done.

Can be frozen prior to baking and then bake at 350° for 30 - 35 minutes. Can also be frozen, after baked. To reheat, do not defrost. Place frozen mushroom patties directly into the oven for 7 - 10 minutes at 350°.

Recipe can be divided in half.

Note

Any leftover filling can be frozen and used at another time, or it can be used as a filling for pita bread or for crêpes.

* My mother preferred to prepare the vegetables with a grater. In testing this recipe, we used the food processor to chop the vegetables. It was faster and the consistency remained the same. I can just hear Ma saying, "It's the modern generation...!"

Onion Knishes
makes 18 - 24

Ingredients
1 lb. puff dough
5 large onions
2 eggs
2 tsp. oil
2 Tbsp. matzo meal
2 Tbsp. Corn Flakes (crushed)
salt and pepper, to taste
☞ approx. 9" x 12" Pyrex dish

Directions
Cut the dough into 4 equal pieces. Roll dough on floured board until it is as thin as tissue paper. Set aside.

Chop onions very finely. Add eggs, oil, matzo meal, crushed Corn Flakes, salt and pepper. Spread filling on each quarter and roll into logs about 16" - 18" long.

Bake for 5 minutes at 400°. Reduce the heat to 350° and bake for 40 minutes or until golden brown.

Remove from oven, cool and cut on the bias (diagonally) at 3" intervals.

Can be frozen. To reheat, do not defrost. Preheat oven to 400° and warm for 20 minutes.

Ven es kumt arine der hunger durch di tir, fleet arroys di libe durch di fenster.
When hunger comes through the door, love flies out the window.

Potato Knishes
makes 9 dozen

Ingredients
1 lb. puff dough
7$\frac{1}{2}$ lbs. potatoes
4 onions
$\frac{1}{2}$ cup oil
$\frac{1}{2}$ cup flour
$\frac{1}{4}$ cup water
salt and pepper, to taste
☛ approx. 9" x 12" Pyrex dish or cookie sheet

Directions
Prepare filling first. Peel, wash and boil potatoes until soft and set aside. Stew onions in half of the oil and all of the water on a low to medium flame until golden brown (about 5 minutes). Add the onion mixture to the boiled potatoes and then mash. Add salt and pepper to taste. Divide into three parts and set aside.

Divide dough into 3 equal parts and roll out each section on a floured board, as thinly as possible. Spread mashed potato mixture evenly over surface ($\frac{1}{8}$" thick).

Roll each of the 3 parts of the dough with their mixture into logs 1$\frac{1}{2}$" in circumference. Slice into $\frac{1}{2}$" knishes and place on greased cookie sheet or Pyrex dish, flat side down.

Bake for 20 - 25 minutes at 350° or until golden brown.

Can be frozen before or after baking. To reheat, do not defrost. Place on a lightly oiled cookie sheet and bake for 30 - 35 minutes at 350° or until golden brown.

Potato Kugel

serves 12 - 15

Ingredients
6 potatoes
1 onion
3/4 cups matzo meal
salt and pepper, to taste
2 eggs
1/4 cup oil + 1/4 cup oil
☛ large mixing bowl filled with cold water
and approx. 9" x 12" Pyrex dish

Directions
Preheat oven to 350°.

Peel and wash potatoes and place in bowl with cold water. Grate potatoes and onion on the wide side of the grater. Rinse, strain and then grate on the fine side of the grater.

Add matzo meal, eggs, salt and pepper. Consistency should be fluffy. Place potato, onion mixture in oiled Pyrex dish (use 1/4 cup). Glaze with balance of oil (1/4 cup).

Bake, uncovered, for 50 - 55 minutes or until golden brown. Check bottom of the kugel to make sure it is done. Cut into 2" squares.

This recipe is parve although it is usually served with meat.

Ein handt vasht di andereh.
One hand washes the other.

Recently, when Phil and I were in Israel we spent time with the Schreiber family. Schmiel, Marlene's dad, is a very special gentleman with a terrific memory.

During our Shabbat dinner, he mentioned that my mother was a super **Balabostah** (good housekeeper) and a wonderful cook. He also added that she was a very caring and good natured person.

Then he told us about one of Ma's dishes that she made way back in 1924. It was just before Leah's sister, Matalla Sicherman, was to leave for New York and Ma prepared a potato kugel for her. Schmiel emphatically described the kugel as **tam genaiden** (a taste of heaven) and that **se lickt mir noch es tam in moyle** (I can still savor the taste in my mouth).

Marlene's brother, Marvin, who knew about the cookbook and took pride in his father's ability to recall these episodes, suggested that if I stayed around long enough, Schmiel would probably give me the recipe. Phil and I decided that we would leave this for our next visit, or if I encountered any difficulty while testing the potato kugel recipe that I already had.

But Schmiel's clear memory of Ma's dish and the **Shabbat** with the Schreibers was certainly a highlight of our stay in Jerusalem.

Varenekes
makes 5 dozen

Filling ingredients
5 lbs. potatoes
4 onions (chopped)
2 - 3 Tbsp. oil
salt and pepper, to taste

Dough ingredients
6 eggs
1 Tbsp. salt
2 cups flour

☞ approx. 20 quart pot and large glass bowl

Directions
Prepare filling first. Boil and mash potatoes. Stew onions in water and oil. Remove 3 Tbsp. of stewed onions and set aside for later. Add the rest of stewed onions to the potatoes. Set aside.

Prepare dough by rolling out on floured board. Use a glass (upside down) to cut round circles in the dough. Use a tablespoon of filling in each circle, fold in half and pinch together. It should resemble a half circle.

A
The varenekes can be frozen at this point. When ready to cook, remove from freezer, defrost and continue as if you had just prepared the varenekes. Do not refreeze after cooking.

B
To prepare fresh fill pot half-full with water and 1 tsp. salt. Bring to a boil and then drop the varenekes into the boiling water. Boil for 5 - 7 minutes. When varenekes are ready, they will rise to the top of the pot. If not, boil for an additional 2 - 3 minutes.

Remove from stove and coddle with 1 cup cold water, while still boiling. Drain and place into a large glass bowl. Set aside. Add the reserve stewed onions and serve.

C

Can be frozen after varenekes have been cooked but do not add the stewed onion mixture. To reheat, defrost, cover and warm in oven on medium heat. Prepare a fresh mixture of onion, water and oil and pour over varenekes just prior to serving.

Recipe can be divided in half.

Ma started to make varenekes at the age of twelve. My grandmother was sickly and the girls had to help with the household chores (there were three girls). Aunt Mathilda, the oldest, left to go to America when she was 18 years old because she wanted more out of life than what she saw in the **schtetel** *(village). It was most fortunate for the Schiff family, because it was Mathilda who worked in the United States and saved up enough money for the entire family to emigrate to America.*

By the time the necessary arrangements were made, immigration laws had changed and entry into the United States was prohibited. However, Aunt Mathilda was undaunted. She contacted distant cousins in Montreal and, with their help, her persistence and determination resulted in the entire Schiff family leaving Boryslav, Poland, to come to Montreal, Canada. However, it took twelve years for the family to be reunited.

❧

Steven Silver returned home from school one day and my mother was making varenekes. Steven, who is immaculate, fastidious and squeamish, looked at her with complete shock and said: "You make them with your hands?! How will I ever eat them again?". Fortunately he got over it and ate varenekes for many years after.

Vegetable Fried Rice

serves 4 - 6

Ingredients
2 cups long grain rice
salt and pepper, to taste
1 Tbsp. garlic powder
2 carrots
2 celery stalks
1 onion
1 lb. mushrooms
1 green pepper
1 red pepper
1 Tbsp. oil
2 Tbsp. soya sauce
☞ approx. 15 quart pot, covered Pyrex dish and medium-size sauce pan

Directions
Prepare rice according to package. Set aside.

Stew onion in oil and a drop of water over a medium flame for 2 - 3 minutes or until golden brown. Wash vegetables and chop into small pieces. Add to the stewed onion. Add salt and pepper, to taste. Stew on a low flame for 15 - 20 minutes until soft. Stir occasionally. When tender, allow to cool for a few minutes.

Mix cooked rice and stewed vegetables together. Add soya sauce and garlic powder and heat just prior to serving.

Can be frozen.

Baked Apples

serves 8

Ingredients
8 MacIntosh apples
$1/2$ cup gingerale
$1/8$ cup cinnamon
☞ Pyrex dish

Directions
Remove half the core of the apples. Pour a little gingerale into cored apples and sprinkle with a dash of cinnamon .

Bake for 40 minutes at 350°, or until soft.

Josie's favourite!

Yeder mentsh hot zein pekel.
Every person has his own load to carry.

Cookies

(plain or with a variety of fillings)
makes 5 dozen

Dough ingredients
3 cups flour
3 eggs
1/2 cup oil
2 Tbsp. shortening
4 tsp. baking powder
juice from 1 lemon
juice from 1 orange
1 Tbsp. whiskey, scotch or rye

Filling ingredients
maraschino cherries, enough to fill each cookie
or
1/4 cup jam (preferably raspberry)
or
2 Tbsp. walnuts (chopped)
2 Tbsp. cocoa + 2 Tbsp. cinnamon + 2 Tbsp. sugar
or
1/4 cup sugar + 1/4 cup cinnamon

☛ cookie sheet, lightly greased

Eynem dacht zich az by yenem lacht zich.
The grass is always greener.

Directions

Prepare dough and refrigerate. Prepare filling of your choice. Set aside.

Preheat oven to 350°.

Remove dough and roll out on floured board until about $1/2$" in thickness. Use a glass (upside down) to form round shapes (2" in diameter). Place on oiled cookie sheet. Use the balance of the dough to reroll for additional cookies.

For maraschino cherry filling, place cherry on top of the circle and wrap around leaving the top open.

For jam filling, do not use glass, simply roll dough and spread jam. Roll (like rolly polly) and cut every $1/2$". Place on oiled cookie sheet on the flat side. (Should look like a circle with a line running through it).

Repeat above procedure for chopped walnut, cocoa, cinnamon and sugar mixture and for sugar and cinnamon mixture, as well.

Place in the oven and bake for 15 - 20 minutes until golden brown.

While testing this recipe, Stella and I made the dough but varied the fillings. Therefore, it is difficult to say how many cookies there are for each variety. In total, we managed to produce 5 dozen cookies with this amount of dough.

Nay iz getrei.
New is true.

Carrot Pudding

Gefilte Fish

Honey Cake

Carrot Tzimmes

Kreplach

Potato Latkes

Haman Taschen

Charoset

Cheese Soufflé

Chremsel (Bubalah)

Cold Beet Borsht

Fried Matzo

Matzo Farfel

Passover Bagel

Potato Latkes Made with Cooked Potatoes

Sponge Cake

Corn Meal Muffins

Cottage Cheese Knaidlach

Cheese Blintzes

Shabbat

Holiday Treats

Light Lunches and Pastas

Salads, Sauces and Soups

Vegetables

Fish

Poultry

Meats

Desserts

Odds 'n' Ends

Many of these delicacies are served on Shabbat and on holidays. Because these are special occasions, they should be observed in a manner different from the rest of the year.

Shabbat *and holidays have become associated with certain foods. During **Rosh Hashanah**, the Jewish New Year, Jews exchange wishes to one another for a sweet year. Thus, during the ceremonial meal on the eve of Rosh Hashanah, it is customary to eat sweet apples dipped in honey, sweet carrots, tzimmes and honey cake.*

Succoth, *the Festival of Booths, is marked by serving dried figs and dates. On **Chanukah**, the Festival of Lights, candles are lit for eight days and latkes, fried in oil are prepared to celebrate the miracle of the oil lamp that burned for eight days on practically no oil.*

*On **Purim**, we eat Haman Taschen, a triangular shaped pastry, stuffed with raisins and nuts or poppy seeds. The pastry is supposed to represent the villainous Haman's triangular hat.*

Pesach (Passover) *is a festive holiday during which Jews recount the exodus of our ancestors, led by Moses from Egypt and the oppression of the Pharaohs. Since there was no time to spare for the dough of bread to rise through fermentation, Passover is known as "The Festival of Unleavened Bread". Therefore, all products made with yeast and flour are removed from the home and we only eat foods made without these staples. Matzo is, of course, unleavened bread.*

Shavuot *commemorates the event of Moses receiving the Ten Commandments from G-d on Mount Sinai. Specific parts of the Torah (the Pentateuch) are read in Synagogue, and the Ten Commandments are recited. The customary meal amongst Ashkenazi Jews consists of dairy products. This is because the purity of the Torah is likened to the purity of milk.*

Rosh Hashanah

Carrot Pudding
serves 12 - 14

Ingredients
1 cup brown sugar
1 cup oil
4 eggs
2 cups carrots (cooked, drained and mashed)
2 cups all purpose flour or matzo meal *
1/2 tsp. salt
2 tsp. baking powder
2 tsp. baking soda
2 tsp. lemon juice
1/2 tsp. cinnamon (optional)
12 oz. can crushed pineapple (drained, optional)
☞ approx. 10" spring form pan

Directions
Preheat over to 375°.

Mix all of the above ingredients together. Place ingredients into lightly greased spring form pan and bake for 50 - 60 minutes. Use a toothpick to check if the pudding is dry. Allow it to cool and then remove from pan.

Can be frozen.

* Matzo meal can be used, but must be measured until consistency is right (approximately 3 cups).

Vi tsvey, iz er a driter.
Where there's two, he'll soon be a third (busy-body).

Gefilte Fish
makes 60 loaves

Ingredients
10 lbs. minced doré *
10 lbs. minced white fish *
6 stalks celery
3 onions
6 carrots
4 parsley roots
2 scallions
salt, sugar and pepper, to taste
6 eggs
2 cups matzo meal
$1/4$ - $1/2$ cup water
☛ approx. 20 - 25 quart pot

Es vet zich oyshelyn biz tsu der khasineh.
It will heal in time for your wedding (it's not as bad as it seems).

Directions

Grind fish with celery. Add eggs to fish with the matzo meal and water (forming a sticky consistency). Make oval shaped balls (approximately 3" x 2") and set aside.

Layer pot with the bones of the fish, onions, 4 carrots, scallions and parsley roots. Fill the pot with water to the halfway mark. Let the water boil and then drop the oval loaves of fish into the boiling water. Lower flame, cover and simmer for 2 hours. Taste and add salt, pepper and a dash of sugar. Keep checking and reduce heat again.

Add additional whole carrots. When fish is cooled and ready to serve cut last 2 carrots into slices and place on top of each loaf of fish. Serve on a bed of lettuce with *chrain* (horseradish). This recipe can be cut in half without any problem.

Cannot be frozen. Recipe can be cut in half for 30 loaves.

* Don't forget to ask for the bones when purchasing the fish. You'll need them for the stock.

*This sounds like an enormous amount of fish, however, Ma made fish for the entire family as well as some friends on **Rosh Hashanah** and **Pesach**. I might add, though, that we never had any leftovers. In fact, many times we had to cut the loaves in half so that some of the family could have seconds and first time visitors could have "just a taste".*

Honey Cake
serves 25 - 30

Dry ingredients
1 cup sugar
1 tsp. baking soda
3 cups flour (sifted)
3 tsp. baking powder

Liquid ingredients
1 cup white natural honey
$3/4$ cup instant coffee (1 tsp. + $3/4$ water)
$1/2$ cup oil
2 Tbsp. whiskey, scotch or rye
6 eggs (separated)

☞ approx. 9" x 12" Pyrex dish, lined with waxed paper

Es zich on eyder di kleyneh kimen on;
ti zich on eyder di grosseh kimen on.

Fill your stomach before the youngsters arrive;
clothe yourself before they grow older.

Directions

Separate eggs, beat egg whites and set aside. Mix dry ingredients and set aside. Mix liquid ingredients and set aside.

Preheat oven to 375°.

Beat egg yolks and slowly add $1/3$ dry ingredients, alternating with $1/3$ liquid ingredients until all ingredients have been combined. Fold in beaten egg whites gently. Place entire batter in Pyrex dish which has been lined with waxed paper.

Bake for 10 minutes. Lower oven to 350° and continue to bake for an additional 30 minutes.

Test with a toothpick to see if cake is dry and ready. If it is not completely ready, continue to bake for an additional 10 - 15 minutes, testing every 5 minutes. Turn oven off and allow cake to cool by keeping the oven door open for approximately 20 minutes.

Turn cake over onto a towel and remove the waxed paper while the cake is still warm.

Can be frozen.

Excellent! Nice and fluffy.

Carrot Tzimmes

Ingredients
3 Tbsp. oil
4 cups raw carrots (sliced)
3 Tbsp. fresh orange juice
salt, to taste
$1/4$ tsp. ginger (optional)
4 Tbsp. honey
3 sweet potatoes
1 lemon
1 cup stewed prunes (optional)

Directions
Mix all ingredients together, cover and cook over low heat for 25 minutes.

Can be frozen. To reheat, defrost, cover and bake in oven for about 10 minutes. Sprinkle with cinnamon (optional).

Finif finger oif eyn handt un nit einer vackst glaych.
Five fingers on one hand and each one grows differently.

Yom Kippur
Breaking the Fast

Stella helped Clara and me with our first Breaking the Fast after Ma passed away. She knew it would be difficult for us and prepared a wonderful meal. The table was set beautifully and the food was delicious and appealing. It was almost as if Ma had been there to supervise.

When we thanked Stella and complimented her, she replied by saying, "I had a very good teacher". Stella really helped make a particularly difficult day, much easier.

Once again, thanks so much, Stella!

Kreplach

(dumplings)

makes 8 dozen

Filling ingredients
4 onions

2 Tbsp. water

1/2 cup oil

1 egg

salt and pepper, to taste

1 whole chicken (boiled, boneless, skinned and cubed)

1 lb. chicken livers

Dough ingredients
2 cups flour

4 eggs

1 Tbsp. salt

cold water, enough to fill half of the broken egg shell 3 times

☞ approx. 20 quart pot

Vi men bet zich ois, azoi schluft men.

You've made your bed, now lie in it.

Directions

Prepare filling first by stewing onions in oil and water until soft and golden brown (about 10 minutes). Remove 4 Tbsp. and set aside. Rinse chicken livers in cold water and add to onions. Continue to stew for an additional 20 minutes until done. Add chicken cubes and continue to cook for an additional 5 minutes. Cool and then grind on the fine cycle of the meat grinder. Add eggs and mix well. Add salt and pepper to taste. Mix and set aside.

To prepare dough mix all dough ingredients together and roll out on a floured board. Cut into 2" x 2" squares. Fill each square with approximately 1 tsp. of filling and fold to form a triangle. Fold the corners in once again and pinch ends together. Make sure there are no openings or the filling will fall out when boiled.

Fill pot half full with water and a pinch of salt. Bring to a boil. Drop kreplach into boiling water and stir gently to keep the kreplach from sticking together. Lower flame, cover and cook for 10 minutes. Remove the pot from the stove, add cold water to the pot to stop the boiling process and then strain.

If serving kreplach as a side dish add the reserve 4 Tbsp. of onions to the dish and serve. If adding kreplach to chicken soup do not add the onions.

Can be frozen. To reheat, defrost and place in a covered Pyrex dish. Place in the oven on medium heat for approximately 20 minutes. Add or delete oil, onion and water mixture depending on how the kreplach are being served.

Elaine's favourite! Ma's labour of love.

Chanukah

Potato Latkes
(potato pancakes)
makes 16

Ingredients
5 medium-size potatoes
$\frac{1}{2}$ cup matzo meal
3 eggs
salt, pepper and garlic powder, to taste (approx. $\frac{1}{8}$ tsp.)
2 onions (optional)
$\frac{1}{4}$ cup oil
☛ 2 large mixing bowls (1 filled with ice cold water)
and approx. 12" fry pan

Directions
Peel and wash potatoes and place in mixing bowl with ice cold water.
This will keep the potatoes from turning grey. Grate potatoes on wide
side of grater and then rinse thoroughly. Grate a second time on the fine
side of the grater. Add eggs, matzo meal, salt, pepper and garlic powder.
Heat fry pan on high and add oil, brown chopped onions (optional) and
then place Tbsp. size drops of batter into fry pan. Fry 2 - 3 minutes on
each side. Remove from pan and place on paper towel to drain excess oil.

Ma had to use a grater and muscle power. I used a blender and then
progressed to a food processor. All three work very well.

Note
The key to making tasty, "aesthetically pleasing" latkes is to work
quickly. Latkes should be as white as possible.

Serve fresh with apple sauce.

Purim

Ma always made **Haman Taschen**, with both prune and poppy seed fillings for the entire family. However, she always took notes on who in the family preferred the prune and who liked the poppy seed. She made sure that everyone was satisfied and indeed they were. In the last few years when she spent a good deal of her time in the kitchen, she added many people to the list of who received her **shalach monis**. The list grew to include the Briskins, and her physician Dr. Laurence Green, whom she respected immensely. She also included my sister Clara's friends - the Barons and the Wexlers, and my friends and extended family - the Zieglers, the Garmaises, the Herschorns, the Fraenkels and the Kussners. She even sent some to our dear Rabbi Poupko at Beth Israel - Beth Aaron Congregation.

I was responsible for the deliveries. This meant that not only did I courier these goodies to Ian in Princeton, New Jersey; Josie and the Zieglers in Toronto and Joel in Providence, Rhode Island, but I also became a delivery girl! My local deliveries criss-crossed the city.

In retrospect, I realize just how much pleasure was exchanged between my mother and the recipients of her goodies. As a result, I have chosen to continue with this tradition.

Good things come in small packages.

Haman Taschen

poppy seed filling and 2 batches of dough makes 9 1/2 dozen
prune filling and 1 batch of dough makes 6 1/2 dozen

Dough ingredients

3 eggs
2 Tbsp. orange juice
2 Tbsp. lemon juice
1 Tbsp. whiskey, scotch or rye
4 tsp. baking powder
2 oz. shortening
1/2 cup oil
1 cup sugar
3 cups flour

Poppy seed filling ingredients

12 oz. poppy seeds
1 cup walnuts (chopped)
3 - 4 Social Tea Biscuits
3 Tbsp. honey
1 apple (peeled and grated)
1/2 cup golden raisins

Prune filling ingredients

12 oz. pitted prunes
1/2 cup walnuts (optional)
1 apple (peeled and grated)
1/2 cup golden raisins
1 Tbsp. honey
2 Social Tea Biscuits

Directions

Prepare dough first and refrigerate for 10 - 15 minutes. Sift the dry ingredients together and then add the rest of the ingredients. Cover and refrigerate for 10 - 15 minutes.

Preheat oven to 350° then prepare fillings.

Poppy seed filling

Boil poppy seeds for 5 minutes and strain with cold water. Grind all ingredients together in a meat grinder except for the honey and the apple which is folded in gently with a spatula at the end.

Prune filling

Grind all ingredients together in a meat grinder except for the honey and the apple which is folded in gently with a spatula at the end.

Roll dough on floured board and then use a glass about 2" in diameter to cut circles (upside down). Fill with poppy seed or prune filling and then fold 3 sides of the circle into the centre to form triangles.   Place on lightly oiled cookie sheet.

Bake for 20 - 30 minutes or until golden brown.

Can be frozen.

Note

Ma used to close the centres completely when preparing the poppy seed haman taschen and she left the centres slightly open when preparing the prune-filled haman taschen so that we were able to identify the varieties without any problem. The majority of the family preferred prune-filled!

Bind mich oyf alla feer, un varf mich tzvishen aygenah.
Blood is thicker than water.

Pesach

Charoset
serves 6 -8

Ingredients
1/2 cup ground walnuts
2 Tbsp. honey
1/4 tsp. cinnamon
2 Tbsp. red wine
2 Red Delicious apples (cored and grated)
juice from 1/2 fresh lemon

Directions
Grind all ingredients together. Adjust to suit taste.

Vos vet zein mit kol Yisroal, vet zein mit mir.
Whatever happens with the people of Israel happily will be my lot as well.

Cheese Soufflé
serves 6 - 8

Ingredients
1 cup milk
1/4 cup sugar
4 eggs (separated)
pinch of salt
2 tsp. vanilla
1 1/2 lbs. cottage cheese
2 19 oz. cans crushed pineapple (drained)
☛ approx. 8" x 6" x 4" deep dish Pyrex dish

Directions
Preheat oven to 350°.

Beat egg whites and set aside. Cream cheese with egg yolks and sugar.
Mix in milk, salt and vanilla. Fold in stiffly beaten egg whites and set
aside. Layer the bottom of Pyrex dish with half of the pineapple and then
gently pour cheese batter over bottom layer. Cover with other half of fruit
and bake for 1 hour. When ready turn oven to off and cool with oven door
open for about 20 - 25 minutes. Expect soufflé to settle a bit.

Alternate method
Use all of the fruit to cover the bottom of the Pyrex dish to form a thicker
bottom half.

Serve hot with sour cream or yogurt and fresh berries.

Chremsel (Bubalah)

(pancake)

serves 4

Ingredients

4 eggs (separated)
1/4 cup whole milk *
2 Tbsp. matzo meal
sweet butter, enough for frying *
☛ approx. 9" round fry pan

Directions

Beat egg whites until stiff and set aside. Beat egg yolks until thick. Stir in milk, add matzo meal and then gently fold mixture into egg whites. Heat butter in fry pan and then gently drop in mixture. Lower flame to medium and then flip over after 2 - 3 minutes.

Sprinkle with sugar prior to serving.

* When I was growing up, my mother used butter and whole milk. Because of the nutritional information available to us today, vis-à-vis fat, I use 1% milk and margarine whenever possible.

Vi men leygt dem kranken tut im alts vey.
No matter where you place the sick person, he's still in pain.

Cold Beet Borscht

Ingredients
4 medium-size beets (fresh)
8 cups water
1 Tbsp. fresh lemon juice
1/2 cup sugar
1 egg
salt, to taste
☞ approx. 20 quart pot

Directions
Peel beets. Slice 2 beets like potato chips, making 2 cups and shred the other 2 beets with a fine shredder, making another 2 cups. Bring water and beets to a boil. Lower flame and let simmer for 20 minutes. Beat egg with a dash of salt and set aside. Add lemon juice and sugar and then let cool. Once cooled, add beaten egg.* Taste, adjust with more lemon, salt and/or sugar.

* Cool borscht prior to adding the egg. If it is added while the borscht is still hot, it will curdle.

Serve with boiled potatoes and sour cream. Delicious!

Fried Matzo
serves 2 - 3

Ingredients
5 matzo slices
3 eggs (beaten)
salt
oil or butter, enough to cover matzo (approx. $\frac{1}{2}$ cup)
4 cups boiling water, enough to absorb 5 matzo slices (approx. 4 cups)
☞ approx. 9" fry pan (deep, if possible)

Directions
Break matzo into small pieces. Boil water and pour over matzo.
Let stand for 3 - 4 minutes. Drain and then discard water. Add beaten
eggs and salt to matzo.

Pour oil into deep fry pan and heat. Drop one piece of matzo into oil.
If it sizzles then the oil is hot enough. Add the rest of the matzo/egg
mixture. Keep turning with a spoon on medium heat until golden brown
(about 3 - 5 minutes). Remove from oil and serve with salt or sugar.

*Whenever my mother felt like eating something different, she made fried
matzo and ate it with jam. She did this year-round.*

Az men vet farteg zein mit allemen, vet men kumen far mir.
When he (the angel of death) is through with everyone else
will he then come for me.

Matzo Farfel
serves 16 - 20

Ingredients
3 cups matzo farfel (uncooked)
2 eggs
2 Tbsp. hot, liquid chicken soup (if using powder, prepare as directed)
16 oz. mushrooms
3 carrots
1 red pepper
1 green pepper
$1/2$ medium-size turnip
3 celery stalks
salt and pepper, to taste
1 onion
garlic powder
2 Tbsp. oil
2 scallions
☞ approx. 10" x 16" cookie sheet

Directions
Grate all of the vegetables on the coarse side of the grater and then stew with 1 Tbsp. of oil until soft (about 15 - 20 minutes). Stir occasionally, alternating from hot to low flame. Add salt, pepper and garlic. Set aside.

Spread dried farfel on cookie sheet, covered with 1 Tbsp. of oil. Beat eggs and mix into farfel. Add salt and pepper and then put into oven at 350° until dry (about 15 - 20 minutes). Make sure to keep stirring every 5 minutes to avoid clumping. When farfel is completed immediately add chicken soup and then add to soft vegetable mixture. Cool for 5 minutes.

Can be frozen. To reheat defrost and then add a drop of liquid chicken stock. Place in the oven, covered, on medium heat for about 15 minutes.

To double this recipe, prepare recipe twice rather than doubling the ingredients and making it once.

Passover Bagel
serves 12

Ingredients
2 cups matzo meal
salt, to taste
1 tsp. sugar
1 cup water
$1/2$ cup oil
4 eggs
☛ approx. 9" x 12" cookie sheet

Directions
Mix matzo meal, salt and sugar. Set aside. Bring oil and water to a boil. Add to matzo meal mixture. Beat in eggs 1 at a time (make sure you are stirring constantly or the eggs will scramble). Let mixture stand for 15 minutes. Oil hands and then shape mixture into 2" - 3" rolls. Make an indentation in the centre of the roll with your thumb and place on a greased cookie sheet. These should look like incomplete doughnuts.

Bake at 400° for 30 minutes or until golden brown. If not golden brown after 30 minutes, it may require an additional 10 - 12 minutes of baking.

Best eaten hot from the oven. Must be eaten fresh.

Vos veyniker men fregt, alts gezinter.
The less you ask, the healthier.

74

Potato Latkes
(made with cooked potatoes)
serves 8 - 10

Ingredients
12" fry pan
6 medium-size potatoes (boiled and mashed)
2 eggs
salt, pepper, to taste
2 Tbsp. oil + oil for frying
1 onion (chopped)
☞ 12" fry pan and 2 large mixing bowls (1 filled with ice cold water)

Directions
Peel, wash and boil potatoes with salt. Mash and set aside. Stew onion in oil and a drop of water. Mix with mashed potatoes and add salt and pepper to taste. Beat eggs and add to potato mixture. Heat oil in fry pan and when sizzling place mixture (2 Tbsp. per latke) into fry pan. Fry 2 - 3 minutes on each side on medium heat. Remove from pan and place on paper towel to drain excess oil.

Do not freeze.

Note
Can be served year-round.

Usually served with cold borscht.

Sponge Cake
serves 12 - 15

Ingredients for Passover
12 eggs
1 1/2 cups cake meal
2/3 cup potato starch
2 Tbsp. white wine
juice from 1 medium-size lemon (with rind)
2 Tbsp. oil
2 cups sugar

Year-round ingredients
12 eggs
3 cups flour (sifted) instead of cake meal
4 tsp. baking powder instead of potato starch
2 Tbsp. whiskey, scotch or rye instead of wine
juice from 1 medium-size lemon (with rind)
2 Tbsp. oil
2 cups sugar
1/2 tsp. cream of tartar

☞ approx. 9" x 4" round pan with hole in the centre

Passover directions
Separate egg whites and yolks and set aside. Beat egg whites with 1 cup of sugar until fluffy. Set aside. Beat egg yolks, wine, balance of the sugar, oil and lemon juice. Blend the two mixtures together. Gently add the cake meal and potato starch to the batter. Beat on low speed.

Preheat oven to 375°.

Pour batter into pan and bake for 10 minutes. Lower oven temperature to 350° and continue to bake for 45 minutes or until ready (it may need an additional 5 -10 minutes of baking time). Test with a toothpick to make sure that the cake is dry. When ready, turn oven off, open oven door and allow cake to cool inside the oven for 30 minutes. Remove and turn upside down on a wire rack to remove from cake pan. The cake should come out easily.

<u>Year-round directions</u>

Separate egg whites and yolks and set aside. Beat egg whites with cream of tartar and 1 cup of sugar until fluffy. Set aside. Beat egg yolks, liquor, balance of the sugar, oil and lemon juice. Blend the two mixtures together. Gently add the sifted flour and baking powder to the batter. Beat at low speed.

Continue to follow the instructions for Passover Sponge Cake.

When my mother met the Zieglers she immediately adored them. The feeling was mutual. Basically, she had an important role to fill - to keep Cleve happy and well-fed when he arrived in Montreal, to complete his residency.

*As I mentioned before, Ma loved to share her goodies with the people who meant so much to her. She began yet another tradition, the tradition of sending the Zieglers a sponge cake for **Pesach**.*

The year that Ma passed away, I felt it would be very meaningful to carry on this tradition because I too, am very fond of them.

Hence, the saga began...

*I had never made a sponge cake before, but as my mother would say, "If you can read, then you can cook and bake". Well, it took only four tries to produce the cake that had any resemblance to the sponge cake I remembered. However, with much desire and some effort, I finally succeeded! The first three cakes were discarded immediately. The expression, **"Es hot mein Baba's tam!"** ("It's tasteless, it's got my grandmother's taste - none!") seemed most appropriate at that time. Hopefully, this year it will be a snap!*

Shavuot

Corn Meal Muffins
makes 24

Ingredients
1 cup flour
1 cup corn meal
1 cup sugar
3 Tbsp. baking powder
3 Tbsp. margarine or butter (softened)
1 lb. dry cottage cheese
1 cup plain yogurt or buttermilk
4 eggs
☞ 12 cup muffin tin

Directions
Preheat oven to 350°.

Separate eggs and set egg whites aside. Cream egg yolks with sugar and then add margarine and cheese to beaten egg yolk mixture. Set aside. Add baking powder to flour and then sift corn meal and flour alternately into batter. Add yogurt or buttermilk and mix thoroughly. Beat egg whites until stiff and fold into batter. Fill lightly greased muffin tin or paper muffin cups with batter (approximately 1" - 1 1/2" high).

Bake for 20 - 25 minutes or until golden brown. Let cool.

Can be frozen. To reheat, defrost and warm in the oven for a few minutes.

Cottage Cheese Knaidlach

(cottage cheese balls)
makes 8 - 10

Ingredients
1/2 lb. dry cottage cheese
4 Tbsp. matzo meal
1/2 tsp. salt
1 Tbsp. sugar
2 eggs (separated)
☞ approx. 10 quart pot

Directions
Fill pot with water halfway and bring to a boil. Beat egg whites and set aside. Combine all other ingredients in a medium-size bowl and gently fold in egg whites. Place in the refrigerator for 15 minutes.

With wet hands shape balls approximately 2" in diameter and then gently drop balls into boiling water. Cook for 15 minutes.

Serve with sour cream.

Mit a man iber dem yam.
Follow your husband over the sea.

Cheese Blintzes

(crêpes)

makes 15

Filling ingredients

1 lb. dry cottage cheese

2 eggs

1/2 cup sugar

pinch of salt

Batter ingredients

3 eggs

1/4 cup milk

3/4 cup water

1/2 cup flour

1/4 lb. melted butter or 1/2 cup oil, enough to cover fry pan

pinch of salt

Directions

Prepare filling first by mixing cheese, eggs, sugar and salt thoroughly until it forms a sticky consistency. Refrigerate.

Prepare batter by beating eggs with salt. Add flour slowly and gently make a paste using a spatula. Keep mixing until very smooth. Dilute with milk and water slowly and stir. Cover the bottom of an approx. 8" fry pan with oil and heat until very hot. Put enough batter into the fry pan (about 2 Tbsp. as thinly spread as possible) and wait until little bubbles begin to form. Flip over for another few seconds. If necessary, use a fork to release the edges. Turn onto waxed paper. Let cool. Always watch the burner and the batter in order for the blintzes not to burn or to dry. Repeat this oil and batter method until batter is used up.

Fill crêpes with 2 Tbsp. of filling per blintz. Fold 4 times - first the long side, then the short side, then long side and then tuck in the last short side (3" x 1 1/2"). Place on cookie sheet or Pyrex dish - seam side down. Bake at 350° for 15 - 20 minutes, or until golden brown. For crispier blintzes, fry in oil or butter for about 2 minutes on each side.

Crêpes can be frozen separately with waxed paper before baking. Thaw and fill. Do not refreeze.

Alternate ratatouille filling ingredients
1 small can tomato sauce
2 tsp. sugar or 1 packet sugar substitute
1/2 lb. mushrooms (finely chopped)
1 green pepper (cubed)
1/2 cup water
grated mozzarella cheese (optional)

Directions
Stew all ingredients together until soft. Fill blintzes, top with mozzarella or Parmesan cheese and bake at 300° for 10 - 15 minutes.

Serve with strawberry, blueberry, raspberry sauce or jam and sour cream or yogurt. Or fill with ratatouille and top with mozzarella cheese.

I always wanted to learn how to make blintzes. One day, my mother came to my home to show me how to make the batter. It can be tricky and she was a pro in preparation and speed. In order to properly master this technique, I wanted a hands-on approach.

I wanted to prepare the batter and filling myself, place it in the fry pan, and flip the blintze at the appropriate time. But I never did get near the stove, because Ma was demonstrating and she worked quickly. On each attempt, Ma protected me from the dangers of the stove and fry pan by shielding the area with her elbows. All the while, she insisted that I pay attention. I was in my early thirties then, with three children of my own, yet somehow things had not changed. I guess I was still her baby and therefore, still not ready to touch the hot stove.

Years later I purchased a Teflon crêpe maker. It was 100% foolproof. I finally showed Ma the finished blintzes and credited my success to her teaching abilities. She was both surprised and proud and I never did tell her about the crêpe maker!

Bow Ties

Cheese Bagel

Chopped Egg Supreme

Cottage Cheese Latkes

Eggplant Parmesan

Kasha and Bow Ties

Leah's Cheese Cake

Lockshen and Cheese

Salted Lockshen Kugel

Sweet Lockshen Kugel

Melai (Mamaligah)

Miniature Pizzas

Rice Pudding

Salmon Latkes

Spanish Omelette

Dairy Spaghetti

Toasted Bagel "Special"

Shabbat

Holiday Treats

Light Lunches and Pastas

Salads, Sauces and Soups

Vegetables

Fish

Poultry

Meats

Desserts

Odds 'n' Ends

Bow Ties

serves 6

Ingredients

8 oz. package bow tie pasta
$1/2$ cup oil
salt and pepper, to taste
2 onions (chopped)
$1/8$ cup water

Directions

Prepare bow ties as directed on the package. When ready, drain and rinse with cold water.

Stew onions in water and oil until golden brown (about 5 - 7 minutes). When ready, pour over bow ties and mix. Warm over medium flame while stirring. Add salt and pepper to taste.

Can be frozen. To reheat, defrost, cover and place in the oven with a drop of water on medium heat until warm (about 10 -15 minutes).

Frequently when Ma sent Marlene a care package of kasha and bow ties, she remembered that Julius preferred bows ties only - and so he got his care package in a separate container. I know how touched Julius was by this kind gesture.

Der sheester geyt alamole borves.
The shoemaker goes without shoes.

Cheese Bagel
makes 25

Ingredients
1 lb. puff dough (cut into 5 strips 2" x 1½")
see filling for Cheese Blintzes (page 80)
☛ approx. 9" x 12" cookie sheet

Directions
Divide puff dough into five parts and roll out on floured board. Place filling on top of dough and roll like a log. Place lengthwise on a lightly greased cookie sheet and cut into 3" long cheese bagels.

Bake for 20 minutes at 400° or until golden brown.

Can be frozen prior to baking. To reheat, do not defrost, place frozen cheese bagels on a greased cookie sheet and bake at 400° for 30 - 35 minutes or until golden brown.

Delicious with sour cream, raspberry or blueberry sauce or jam!

Drei techter iz nit kein gelechter.
Three daughters is no laughing matter.

Chopped Egg Supreme

serves 4 - 6

Ingredients

6 hard boiled eggs
2 medium-size potatoes (peeled and cooked)
1 Tbsp. oil
1 small onion (finely chopped)
salt and pepper, to taste
$1/8$ tsp. sugar, to taste (optional)

Directions

Mash eggs and potatoes in a medium-size bowl. Add onion, oil, salt and pepper to taste.

Fun ein schtickle holtz ken men machen a malach un a tivel.
From one piece of wood, one can carve an angel or a devil.

Cottage Cheese Latkes

makes 3 dozen

Ingredients

¹/₂ cup flour (sifted)
¹/₂ tsp. baking powder
salt, to taste
3 Tbsp. sugar
¹/₂ cup sour cream
¹/₂ lb. dry cottage cheese
3 eggs (separated)
oil, enough to cover fry pan
☞ approx. 9" round fry pan

Directions

Beat egg whites and set aside. Beat egg yolks and add the rest of the ingredients. Stir until puréed and then fold in egg whites. Cover pan with oil and heat over medium flame. Place about 2 Tbsp. of mixture into hot fry pan. Latkes should be about 3" in diameter. Work quickly so that the latkes do not burn. Brown on both sides. Replenish oil as it is being absorbed. When ready, remove from pan and place on paper towel to absorb excess oil.

Can be frozen but preferably should be eaten fresh.

Great with sour cream!

Leah's Cheese Cake

(mamaligah or melai with cottage cheese)
serves 6

Ingredients

1 lb. cottage cheese
4 eggs
1/4 cup corn meal
1/4 cup flour
1/2 cup sugar
1 tsp. lemon juice
1 Tbsp. margarine (melted)
1/2 cup buttermilk
☛ approx. 9" x 9" Pyrex dish

Directions

Mix all of the ingredients together by hand or with a mix master on low speed until well-blended. Place in a lightly oiled Pyrex dish and bake at 450° for 25 minutes or until golden brown.

Leah sent this to Marlene, explaining it was originally Chana's recipe.

Lockshen and Cheese
(noodles and cheese)
serves 6 - 8

Ingredients
8 oz. box broad noodles
1 lb. dry cottage cheese
2 Tbsp. cinnamon
2 Tbsp. sugar or 2 packets sweetener
raisins (optional)
☞ approx. 10 quart pot

Directions
Prepare noodles as directed on package. Drain and rinse with cold water.
Place noodles back on the stove to warm for a few minutes.

Sprinkle with cinnamon and sugar or sweetener. Top with cottage cheese
and raisins, if desired.

Az men schmirt, furt men.
He who pays the piper, calls the tune.

Salted Lockshen Kugel
(salted noodle pudding)
serves 12 - 15

Ingredients
8 - 10 oz. bag extra-broad noodles
3 onions
4 eggs
salt and pepper, to taste
1 Tbsp. sugar
2 cups Corn Flakes (crushed)
3 Tbsp. oil
☛ approx. 9" x 12" Pyrex dish and 10 quart pot and 9" round fry pan

Directions
Preheat oven to 350°.

Stew onions in oil and water and set aside. Boil noodles and rinse in cold water. Mix all ingredients together except the Corn Flakes crumbs and oil. Pour noodles and other ingredients into oiled Pyrex dish. Sprinkle top with crushed Corn Flakes.

Bake, uncovered, for 30 minutes.

Cover and return to oven for an additional 15 - 20 minutes or until golden brown. Cool and cut in 2" x 2" squares.

Can be frozen. To reheat, defrost, cover and heat in warm oven until hot.

Note
Parve, although usually served with meat.

Murray's favourite!

Sweet Lockshen Kugel
(sweet noodle pudding)
serves 15 - 18

Ingredients
8 - 10 oz. bag extra-broad noodles
4 eggs
12 oz. can crushed pineapple (drained)
1 Tbsp. raspberry jam
1 Tbsp. peach jam
1 tsp. cinnamon
3 Tbsp. oil
1 apple (grated)
$\frac{1}{4}$ cup golden raisins
2 Tbsp. honey
1 cup Corn Flakes (crushed)
☛ approx. 9" x 12" Pyrex dish and 10 quart pot

Directions
Preheat oven to 350°.

Boil noodles and rinse with cold water. Mix everything together, except for the corn flake crumbs. Pour into oiled Pyrex dish. Sprinkle top with crushed Corn Flakes.

Bake, uncovered, for 45 minutes or until golden brown.

Cover and continue to bake for another 15 minutes. This will prevent it from hardening or getting dry. Cut in 2"x 2" squares.

Can be frozen.

Recipe can be divided in half.

My favourite!

Melai (Mamaligah)

serves 9

Ingredients

3 eggs
1 1/2 cup corn meal
1/4 cup sugar
1/4 cup flour (sifted)
2 tsp. baking powder
1/8 tsp. salt
2 Tbsp. lemon juice
2 Tbsp. corn oil
1 1/4 cup buttermilk
☛ approx. 8" x 8" Pyrex dish

Directions

Mix all ingredients together by hand or with a mix master on low speed until well-blended.

Place in a lightly oiled Pyrex dish and bake at 450° for 25 minutes.

Serve hot with sour cream or jam or both.

When this was served I often heard these words of wisdom...
"Az men essed dos far a hundert yoren - ken men lang leben!"
"If one eats this for a hundred years, then one could live a very long life!"

Tip

If ever you are unsure of how much baking powder to use, the equation is:
1 tsp. baking powder to 1 cup flour.

Miniature Pizzas
makes 12

Ingredients
6 English muffins
8 oz. shredded mozzarella cheese (optional)
1 green pepper (cut into small pieces)
$^1/_2$ lb. mushrooms (sliced into small pieces)
8 ozs. pizza sauce
☞ approx. 9" x 12" cookie sheet

Directions
Spread the pizza sauce on top of $^1/_2$ of the English muffin. Stew the green pepper and mushrooms in a drop of water for 5 minutes. Spread the mixture on top of the muffin shell – approximately 2 Tbsp. per muffin. If cheese is used, sprinkle 1 Tbsp. of shredded cheese on top of mixture (enough to cover the surface).

Bake on medium heat for 10 minutes or until cheese melts. If you're not using cheese, bake on medium heat for 5 minutes until muffins are hot.

Can be frozen. To reheat, defrost and warm in oven for 3 - 5 minutes on medium heat. Do not cover.

Er vil mir arynreden a kreynk in boych.
He wants to convince me of the impossible.

Rice Pudding

serves 12

Ingredients

2 cups cooked rice
2 cups milk
$1/4$ tsp. salt
$1/2$ cup sugar
1 Tbsp. butter or oil
2 eggs
1 tsp. lemon juice
$1/2$ tsp. cinnamon
$1/2$ cup raisins
☛ approx. 9" x 12" Pyrex dish

Directions

Preheat oven to 325°.

Combine all ingredients in the order given. Place in greased Pyrex dish and cook for approximately 1 hour or until nicely browned.

A kranker freght men, a gezunter git men.
Ask the sick (if they wish to eat) serve the healthy (without asking).

Salmon Latkes
(salmon patties)
makes 8

Ingredients
1 large can of salmon (approx. 7.5 ozs.)
3 eggs
1/8 cup matzo meal
1/8 cup Special K cereal (crushed)
oil, enough to cover fry pan
1/2 onion (chopped, optional)
☞ large fry pan

Directions
Drain salmon, add eggs, matzo meal and mash with crushed Special K.
The consistency should be soft but not runny.

Cover the fry pan with oil. Test to see if the oil is hot enough by dropping
a drop of mixture into the oil. If it sizzles, it's ready. Sauté onion for a
few minutes.

Drop 1 Tbsp. of mixture into the pan for each latke. Brown on both sides.
Total frying time is about 5 minutes (flip only once). Remove latkes and
place on paper towel to drain excess oil.

*My mother always served salmon latkes with green peas and a mound of
mashed potatoes made with lots of butter. I remember eating them when
recovering from a cold or the flu. I always served salmon latkes to my
kids when Phil was on call at the hospital or when he was out of town.
Just recently Josie mentioned to me that she never really did enjoy that
meal .... I wonder why?*

Spanish Omelette

serves 4

Ingredients
6 eggs (separated)
2 Tbsp. butter or margarine
8 oz. mozzarella cheese (shredded)
1 lb. of mushrooms (cut into small pieces)
2 green peppers (cubed)
2 onions (chopped finely, optional)
1 red pepper (cubed, optional)
1 tomato (cubed, optional)
salt and pepper, to taste
☞ approx. 9" oval fry pan

Directions
Separate eggs. Beat egg whites and set aside. Wash and chop vegetables.
Set aside. Shred cheese and set aside. Place butter in hot fry pan, add
vegetables and stew for 3 - 4 minutes. Stir continuously. Mix egg yolks
with beaten egg whites and add to mixture. Stir for a few minutes. Add
shredded cheese at the end and stir until melted. If dry, add an additional
pat of butter or margarine.

This recipe was first tried on a gas range and so cooking time was much
quicker than on an electric range.

*The Spanish Omelette is actually Phil's recipe. He was puttering in the
kitchen up at the country house and although my mother loved him like a
son, she didn't appreciate his presence in the kitchen. While he was
making this Spanish Omelette, she decided to take a walk *. When she
returned, Phil urged her to taste what he had made. She said she loved it
and from then on, claimed it for herself.*

** As she was leaving, I overheard her say rather quietly, "Too many cooks
in the kitchen" her version of, "Too many cooks spoil the broth".*

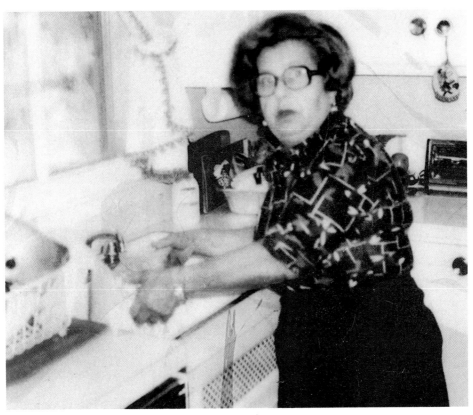

My mother in the kitchen at Trout Lake. It was here that Phil made the famous Spanish Omelette, that Ma eventually claimed for herself.

Dairy Spaghetti

serves 10 - 12

Ingredients

16 oz. box thin spaghetti noodles
2 onions (sliced)
3 Tbsp. parve margarine
3 slices Canadian cheese (orange)
3 tsp. sugar
$1/2$ cup ketchup
☛ approx. 10 quart pot and 9" round fry pan

Directions

Prepare spaghetti noodles as directed on the package. When ready, drain and rinse with cold water. Set aside.

Stew onions in margarine and a little water (just enough to cover pan). Mix ketchup, cheese, sugar and stewed onions and margarine. Stew over low flame for 10 - 15 minutes.

Add mixture to noodles. Mix together and let simmer on low flame for an additional 5 - 7 minutes.

Can be frozen. To reheat, defrost, add a drop of water and a drop of ketchup and simmer on low flame until hot.

Joel's, Cleve's, Elaine's and my favourite!

Er veindt un er koched kreplach.
He complains even though he has reason to celebrate.

Toasted Bagel "Special"

Ingredients
bagel
butter, enough to spread on sliced bagel

Directions
Slice bagel and spread with butter.

Toast in toaster oven until bagel is browned and butter gets runny. Serve hot.

Ma would often tell the story of how when she babysat for our kids while we were on vacation, she could never get Ian to eat. Finally he agreed to have a toasted bagel, but only if it was made to his specifications. She would laugh every time she repeated the story, because here was this little kid telling her how to cook.

Az men hot kinder in di veegan, darf men lozen layten tsufreeden.
People in glass houses shouldn't throw stones.

Chicken Salad

Lettuce and Cucumber Salad

Coleslaw

Potato Salad

Salad Dressing

Sweet 'n' Sour Sauce

Meat Sauce

Bean and Barley Soup

Pea Soup

Cabbage Soup

Shabbat

Holiday Treats

Light Lunches
and Pastas

Salads, Sauces
and Soups

Vegetables

Fish

Poultry

Meats

Desserts

Odds 'n' Ends

In the early Sixties, most people were just beginning to distinguish between eating properly and overeating. My mother was always a step ahead of her time when it came to nutrition, a balanced diet and the benefits of eating lightly.

One Sunday, just prior to our cousins Riva and Jarvis Freedman's engagement, Ma invited them to Montreal to meet the family. They lived in Ottawa and graciously accepted the invitation. I only found out the real story of that evening when I mentioned to Riva, Marlene's sister, that I was writing a cookbook of Ma's recipes. Riva recounted this tale:

Just prior to the prenuptial dinner, Riva informed Jarvis that he was in for the treat of his life and should not eat anything at all on that day, because Chana would be serving a 'meal fit for a king'.

They weren't aware that Ma had modified her menu because it was fashionable to look svelte. Everyone wanted to look like Twiggy.

Riva and Jarvis arrived and sat down to dinner with great anticipation. Soup was served and it was delicious. Then came the salad and that too was delicious. Ma always offered seconds but Jarvis was saving himself for the main course. Surprise! Out came the cheesecake! What a disappointment for the couple who were expecting a banquet.

If Ma were alive today and had known the background information of that meal, she would be beside herself with guilt for sending away two very hungry dinner guests!

Chicken Salad
serves 6

Ingredients
boiled chicken (great way to use up leftovers)
salad (any vegetables that you like)
oil, salt, and pepper, to taste
1 packet sweetener

Directions
Remove skin and bones from chicken and cut into cube-sized bites.
Set aside. Prepare vegetables, add oil, salt, pepper and sweetener, to taste.

Prepare just prior to serving.

Tsu git iz halb narrish.
Always being a do-gooder is somewhat foolish.

Lettuce and Cucumber Salad

serves 4

Ingredients
3 leaves lettuce
1 medium-size cucumber
3/4 cup vinegar
1 tsp. sugar
2 packets sweetener
salt and pepper, to taste

Directions
Mix vinegar, sugar, salt and pepper together in a large bowl. Add lettuce and cucumber. Marinate for several hours.

Can be refrigerated for about one week.

Dos epele falt nit vayt fun beymele.
The apple doesn't fall far from the tree.

This was Murray's favourite dish. Murray and my mother had a very special relationship built on mutual love, admiration, and affection. They lived next door to each other for 30 years and yet maintained a successful friendship. Murray became the son Mama never had, and though he often teased her, she always knew it was just his way of showing affection.

Shveeger *(mother-in-law), was Murray's nickname for her. Although it can be used in a derogatory sense, we all knew Murray meant it as dear one.*

Murray continually teased my mother about anything and everything - especially her cooking. On many occasions, he told her to take some cooking lessons because she could use all the help she could get. But whenever he said that, she interpreted it to mean that it was delicious. She always appreciated the compliment.

Murray had a certain sensitivity that Ma responded to, especially after my father passed away in 1964. He opened his home to her and made her laugh with his gift of turning any situation into a humorous one. But he also had a serious side. After each Seder together, he would always make a toast to my mother. He blessed her with good health and many years of cooking for our Seders. Unfortunately, we lost Murray in a most untimely fashion in 1989. To compound the sadness, Ma was only able to make four more Seders after Murray's passing.

Coleslaw
serves 8 - 10

Ingredients
¹/₂ medium-size cabbage
3 carrots
1 green pepper
¹/₄ cup vinegar
garlic powder, salt and pepper, to taste
¹/₄ cup sugar
red pepper (optional)

Directions
Shred cabbage, should be fine. Shred carrots and green pepper. Add vinegar. Set aside for 15 minutes. Add garlic powder and sugar and salt and pepper, to taste. Refrigerate.

Dem oreman felt shtendik a tog tsu der vokh.
The pauper is always the loser.

Potato Salad

serves 6 - 8

Ingredients
4 potatoes
1 carrot
1 celery stalk
4 Tbsp. mayonnaise
$1/4$ green pepper
$1/4$ red pepper
$1/8$ tsp. pepper
salt, to taste
1 onion (optional)
1 red pimento
☛ large bowl

Directions
Peel, wash and boil potatoes. Drain, cool and cube. Wash other vegetables and chop into small pieces. Mix everything together and place in a large bowl. Add mayonnaise, salt and pepper, to taste. Refrigerate immediately.

Salad Dressing

Ingredients
1 cup oil
$^1/_2$ cup vinegar
1 tsp. garlic powder, to taste
salt and pepper, to taste
1 packet sweetener
salad spice, to taste (optional)
☞ large glass jar

Directions
Mix all ingredients together. Adjust to taste and shake well. Place in a jar and it is ready to serve. Can be refrigerated for about 2 weeks.

This recipe can be doubled, tripled, etc.

Use 1 Tbsp. salad dressing per salad serving.

Beser mit a klugn tsu farliren eyder mit a nar tsu gevinen.
It's better to lose an argument with a wise man
than to win an argument with a fool.

Sweet 'n' Sour Sauce
makes 5 cups

Ingredients
1 Tbsp. vinegar
19 oz. can tomato juice
14 oz. can pineapple tidbits
$1/2$ cup brown sugar
pinch of salt
1 Tbsp. corn starch
$1/2$ cup cold water
☞ approx. 5 quart sauce pan

Directions
Mix corn starch and cold water together and set aside. Mix vinegar, tomato juice, brown sugar and salt. Bring this mixture to a boil, then lower flame and keep stirring.

Gradually add the liquid corn starch mixture to the sauce. Add pineapple tidbits in its own juice at the very end.

Can also be used for cooking dishes that require prepared sweet and sour sauce.

Great with chicken, beef, egg rolls or rice.

Meat Sauce
serves 10 - 12

Ingredients
2 lbs. minced steak

or

1 lb. minced steak + 1 lb. minced veal

2 cloves fresh garlic (crushed)

or

1 Tbsp. garlic powder

1 bay leaf

salt and pepper, to taste

$1/4$ cup oil, enough to cover the pot

19 oz. can tomato juice

19 oz. water

$5^1/2$ oz. can tomato paste

1 medium-size onion (cubed)

19 oz. can tomato sauce

2 packets sweetener

dash of chilies (optional)

2 - 3 Tbsp. liquid chicken stock (optional) *

☞ approx. 15 quart pot

He's lucky that his father was born before him!

Directions

Sauté cubed onion in oil and a drop of water. When the oil is hot, brown the minced meat and garlic. Allow to brown on all sides. Lower flame and stir occasionally. This should take about 5 minutes.

Add tomato juice and equal amount of water. Add the tomato paste, the tomato sauce and the chicken stock. Bring to a boil on a medium flame. Lower flame and continue to simmer. Make sure mixture is still boiling. Add salt, pepper, sweetener, chilies and a bay leaf. Taste and adjust accordingly. Lower flame, cover, and simmer for 2 hours. Stirring every 15 - 20 minutes. Check consistency.

If the sauce is too thick, add water. If the sauce is too thin, then uncover and slightly increase the temperature of the stove for a few minutes. Taste again and adjust. Remove the bay leaf. Turn stove off and cool sauce.

Can be frozen in individual serving containers. To reheat, defrost, add a drop of water and a bit of tomato juice. Heat on medium flame. Stir occasionally until hot (should take about 10-15 minutes).

* As Ma used to say, "Chicken soup can't do any harm, it can only make it better." I recommend using chicken stock as it adds a nice taste to the sauce.

Bean and Barley Soup
serves 8 -10

Ingredients
1 package bean and barley soup mix
2 small potatoes (cut into cubes)
6 small carrots (cup into small pieces)
2 Tbsp. dry chicken stock
1 tsp. oil
3 celery stalks
4 greens of parsley roots
2 quarts water
1 onion
☛ approx. 10 quart pot

Directions
Follow instructions on package of soup mix except delete the salt
(it's much tastier without the additional salt).

Bring 1 quart of water and oil to a boil. Add bean and barley soup mix,
celery and onion. Let simmer over medium to low flame. After one hour,
add the potatoes, carrots and greens and an additional 1 quart of water.

Continue to cook for another hour. Take out greens, onion and celery.

Can be frozen.

Excellent!

Yeder kindt brenght mit zich zayn eigeneh mazel.
Each child brings it's own luck.

Pea Soup
serves 8 -10

Ingredients
1 package split peas
2 potatoes
3 celery sticks
1 onion
1 Tbsp. oil
1 Tbsp. sugar
salt and pepper, to taste
☛ approx. 8 quart pot

Directions
Follow instructions on package of soup mix with the following exceptions: add oil, sugar, onion and celery to water with peas. Bring to a boil, lower flame and cook for 1 hour. Add whole or cut up potatoes.

Continue to cook on low flame for another hour (cooking time is 2 hours in total). Remove onion and celery. Soup should be thick.

Can be frozen.

Helpful hint for soup
If your soups have ever been over-salted, just add a washed, peeled potato to the soup and continue to cook over a low flame until the potato is soft. It will absorb the salt. Remove the potato when the soup is ready. This holds true for the preparation of any foods, although it works best with liquids.

Er macht shabbes far zich alein.
He prepares Shabbat for himself only (selfishly).

Cabbage Soup
(with or without meat)
makes 18 soup servings and 8 meat servings

Ingredients without meat
2 small onions (cubed)
2 small MacIntosh apples (peeled and cubed)
1 tomato (cut into eighths)
1 Tbsp. oil
1 medium-size cabbage (finely shredded)
$1/2$ cup brown sugar
1 cup ketchup
2 19 oz. cans tomato juice
3 cups water
1 cup golden raisins
1 cup honey
salt and pepper, to taste
☛ approx. 20 quart pot

Ingredients with meat
Ingredients are listed in the same order with one exception:
Replace oil with 2 strips of 1 - $1^{1}/4$ lbs. flanken (cut into 8 cubes)

Directions

Layer ingredients in the pot in order given but add only 1 can of tomato juice. Cover and stew over medium flame until soft. Bring to a boil and then lower flame. Simmer for 1 hour.

After 1 hour, add additional water until pot is $^3/4$ full and the other can of tomato juice. Simmer for an additional 1 - 1$^1/2$ hours. During the cooking process, taste, add salt and pepper to taste. While testing, you may need additional brown sugar, raisins and ketchup.

Ma liked this sweet and tangy. Always remember, raisins tend to get sweeter as they are being cooked. Consider this when adding additional sugar. Colour should be reddish-brown.

Can be frozen. To reheat, defrost and add a drop of honey and ketchup, to taste. Place on stove over medium flame until hot.

Note

If meat is being used follow the same directions but add the meat instead of the oil.

Delicious! A meal in itself.

Saichel kimpt noch di yoren.
Wisdom comes with time.

Breaded Cauliflower

Breaded Mushrooms

Carrot Latkes

Cauliflower Latkes

Egg Rolls

Shabbat

Holiday Treats

Light Lunches
and Pastas

Salads, Sauces
and Soups

Vegetables

Fish

Poultry

Meats

Desserts

Odds 'n' Ends

Breaded Cauliflower

makes 25 - 30 pieces

Ingredients
1 medium-size cauliflower
1 cup matzo meal *
¼ cup oil, enough to cover fry pan
garlic powder, to taste
2 eggs (beaten)
salt and pepper, to taste
☞ approx. 9" round fry pan

Directions
Break cauliflower into bite-sized pieces. Wash and dry the cauliflower
and then dip it in the matzo meal, salt, pepper and garlic powder mixture.
Beat eggs and dip breaded cauliflower into mixture.
Repeat this process twice.

Heat oil in fry pan and fry cauliflower bites for 2 - 3 minutes on each side
until crispy. Place on paper towel to remove excess oil and cool.

Best eaten fresh.

* Breadcrumbs can be substituted for matzo meal.

Breaded Mushrooms

makes 14 - 18

Ingredients
½ lb. mushrooms (approx. 14 mushrooms)
1 cup matzo meal or breadcrumbs
½ tsp. garlic powder, to taste
oil, enough to cover fry pan (approx. ⅛ cup)
salt and pepper, to taste
2 eggs (beaten)

Directions
Wash mushrooms in cold water and dry them well. Remove stems, leaving mushrooms whole.

Mix matzo meal, garlic powder, salt and pepper. Dip mushrooms into dry mixture. Dip coated mushrooms into beaten eggs. Dip in dry mixture and eggs again.

Fry mushrooms for about 2 minutes on each side or until golden brown. Place them on a paper towel to remove excess oil and to cool.

Recipe can be doubled for 36 mushrooms.

Meh zol nit gepreevdt veren tsu vos meh ken gevoindt veren.
We should not be tested with things we might have to learn to live with.

Carrot Latkes
makes 36

Ingredients
3 fresh carrots
1/4 cup matzo meal
3 eggs
salt and pepper, to taste
oil, enough to cover fry pan
☞ approx. 9" round fry pan

Directions
Chop carrots. Mix eggs, matzo meal, salt and pepper together and add to the chopped carrots. Consistency should not be sticky or runny, but somewhere in between.

Fry latkes in hot oil. Use 1 tsp. of the mixture for frying in order to make bite sized latkes. Fry until golden brown, turning latkes over only once. Total frying time is about 3 - 5 minutes. Place the latkes on paper towel to remove excess oil and cool.

Note
Use the same amount of eggs as carrots (1 egg = 1 carrot).

Der tog iz noch groyse.
We still have time.

Cauliflower Latkes
makes 9 - 10

Ingredients
1 small cauliflower
1/2 cup matzo meal
2 eggs (beaten)
oil, enough to cover fry pan
salt, pepper and garlic powder, to taste
☞ approx. 10 quart pot and 9" round fry pan

Directions
Fill pot with water, bring to a boil and blanch cauliflower for a few minutes. It should not be too soft. Mash the cauliflower with a hand masher, and then add the salt, pepper and garlic powder to taste. Add the beaten eggs and matzo meal to the mixture.

Cover fry pan with oil and heat until oil is hot. Fry 1 Tbsp. of mixture for each latke. Fry for about 2 minutes on each side or until golden brown. Place the latkes on paper towel to remove excess oil and cool (about 5 minutes).

Best eaten fresh.

Egg Rolls
makes 5$^1/_2$ dozen

Filling ingredients
2 Tbsp. oil
salt and pepper, to taste
1 tsp. garlic powder
1 small, curled cabbage
2 scallions
2 small parsley roots
2 carrots
$^1/_4$ turnip
1 small green pepper
1 small red pepper
2 celery stalks
1 small onion
dash of sugar (optional)
$^1/_2$ cup Corn Flakes (crushed)

Dough ingredients
3 large eggs
$^1/_2$ cup oil
2 cups flour
2 Tbsp. salt

☛ approx. 15 quart pot and 9" round fry pan

Directions

Prepare filling first. Grate vegetables on the wide side of the grater. Stew the vegetables over a medium flame in oil, garlic powder, salt and pepper for about 15 minutes. Taste and add sugar if necessary. After the vegetables are soft, remove from the stove and add the corn flake crumbs to give the mixture a more solid, workable texture. Set aside.

Prepare dough. Mix all the dough ingredients together and knead, until soft. Roll dough out on floured board and cut into 3" strips. Place the filling onto the dough (about 1" wide x 1" high). Roll over once to form a log. Cut roll every 2½". Close both ends by sticking dough together. Fry until golden brown in oiled pan on medium heat. Remove and leave on paper towel until cool.

Can be frozen.

To reheat, do not defrost. Cover and reheat on medium heat in the oven for about 20 minutes.

Dir tochter zog ich, un dir schneer mein ich.
Since I can't say it to my daughter-in-law,
I certainly hope she's listening when I say it to my daughter.

Baked Salmon or Halibut

Pickled Salmon

Marinated Salmon

Stuffed Fillet of Sole

Shabbat

Holiday Treats

Light Lunches
and Pastas

Salads, Sauces
and Soups

Vegetables

Fish

Poultry

Meats

Desserts

Odds 'n' Ends

Baked Salmon or Halibut
serves 4 - 8

Ingredients
4 slices Atlantic salmon

or

4 slices halibut

or

2 slices salmon + 2 slices halibut

1 green pepper

2 tomatoes

3 celery stalks

3 carrots

3 potatoes

1/2 lb. fresh yellow waxed beans or 19 oz. can waxed beans

1/2 lb. fresh green beans (optional)

12 oz. can tomato juice

1/4 cup ketchup

1 Tbsp. oil

☞ approx. 9" x 12" Pyrex dish

Directions
Preheat oven to 350° for about 10 - 15 minutes.

Cut vegetables into small pieces and place them in the Pyrex dish with just enough oil to cover the bottom. Bake, uncovered for 20 - 30 minutes. When the vegetables are almost soft, place the salmon or halibut slices on top of the vegetables and cover with the tomato juice and the ketchup. Return dish to the oven for an additional 30 minutes. Cover for the first 10 minutes. Remove cover and keep basting for the last 20 minutes.

Can be frozen.

Nice when served with spinach and a baked potato. If salmon or halibut slices are large, serve 1/2 slice per person.

Pickled Salmon

(revised version of Marinated Salmon, page130)
serves 12

Ingredients

6 slices Atlantic salmon steaks
or
6 filleted baby Atlantic salmon steaks (with skin)
2 Spanish onions (sliced)

Sauce ingredients

2 cups water
1 cup vinegar
1 cup white sugar
1^1/2 cup ketchup
3 bay leaves
1 handful of pickling spice (approx. 3 Tbsp.)
^{1}/4 tsp. salt

☛ approx. 20 quart pot and 9" x 12" Pyrex dish

Directions

Salt salmon and set aside. Fill the large pot half full of water and add salt.
Bring to a boil and cook salmon in boiling water for 10 minutes. Drain
and set salmon aside and discard the water.

Prepare the sauce by boiling ingredients for 20 minutes. Taste to suit your
palate (sweet or spicy). Put into the Pyrex dish and add the salmon
layering it with the Spanish onion slices. Cool, cover and refrigerate.
Serve cold.

Salmon takes about 4 days for the actual marinating, however, it can be
eaten at any time after having been cooled and refrigerated. Can be stored
in the refrigerator for about 10 days.

Marinated Salmon

serves 4 - 6

Ingredients

4 Atlantic salmon steaks

or

filleted baby Atlantic salmon (with skin)

salt, to taste

3 cups of water

1 onion

2 celery stalks

2 carrots

1 cup of vinegar

1 cup of sugar

pepper, to taste

1 Tbsp. pickling spice

1 bay leaf

☛ approx. 20 quart pot and a 9" x 12" Pyrex dish

A glick hot mir getrophen!
Am I lucky!

Directions

Salt salmon, fill the pot with water halfway and add a pinch of salt. Bring water to a boil and poach the salmon for 4 - 5 minutes. Remove the salmon and discard the water. Set salmon aside.

To prepare marinade make a broth of onion, water, celery, carrots, salt and pepper to taste. Add the vinegar, sugar, pickling spice and bay leaf.

Boil for 20 minutes. Strain and taste. Add salmon to marinade, lower flame and continue to cook (still boiling) for 7 - 10 minutes until flaky. Drain and place salmon in Pyrex dish. Add marinade.

Note

If you prefer to leave the vegetables in the broth while cooking the salmon, the pickling spice MUST BE REMOVED. If you leave the pickling spice in the broth the salmon will turn black.

Serve hot or cold. Can be stored in the refrigerator for about 1 week.

This recipe was given to me by my cousin Marlene. Ma originally gave the recipe to her.

Yeder mentch hot zayn eygenem meshugas.
Every person has his own version of lunacy.

Stuffed Fillet of Sole
serves 6 - 8

Ingredients
6 slices of fillet of sole
1 celery stalk
2 carrots
1 sprig of parsley
2 potatoes
1 green pepper
1 tomato
1 onion
$1/2$ lb. mushrooms (optional)
19 oz. can niblets (optional)
$1/2$ cup ketchup
3 Tbsp. brown sugar
19 oz. can tomato juice
oil, enough to cover dish and dab top of fillets (approx. 1 Tbsp.)

Stuffing ingredients
2 celery stalks (finely chopped)
2 carrots (finely grated)
salt and pepper, to taste
$1/4$ cup Corn Flakes (crushed)
3 Tbsp. flour

Alternative sauce ingredients
12 oz. can vegetarian vegetable soup
6 ozs. water

☛ approx. 9" x 12" Pyrex dish

Directions

Mixing ingredients for stuffing and set aside. Dice all other vegetables and place in greased Pyrex dish.

Bake for 20 minutes, uncovered, on medium heat and keep mixing. Wash fillets and place approximately 2 - 3 Tbsp. of stuffing at one end of each fillet and roll to the other end. Insert a toothpick to keep it from unrolling.

Place stuffed fillets on vegetable mixture – seam side down – and cover with tomato juice, brown sugar and dab with the balance of the oil (about 1^1/$_2$ tsp.) or, if using the alternative sauce, cover with soup and water.

Bake for 30 minutes at 400° and then lower heat to 350°. Bake for an additional 30 minutes, uncovered. Baste every 10 - 15 minutes.

Can be frozen with vegetables and sauce. Seal very tightly.

Serve with baked potato.

Az men zol oyfhengen oyf der vant alemens tsouris,
volt zich yaider aynem gechapt zayn eygns.

If you would hang everyone's troubles on the wall,
everyone would grab for his own.

Chicken Kalochlach

Breaded Chicken Breasts

Chinese Chicken Livers

Chicken Meat Loaf with Vegetables

Chicken Meatballs

Chicken Nuggets

Chicken Wings

Pineapple Chicken

Roast Turkey

Southern Fried Chicken

Shabbat

Holiday Treats

Light Lunches
and Pastas

Salads, Sauces
and Soups

Vegetables

Fish

Poultry

Meats

Desserts

Odds 'n' Ends

Chicken Kalochlach

(chicken meatballs)

makes 20 - 24

Kalochlach ingredients

1 lb. minced chicken

2 eggs

1/4 cup matzo meal

2 Tbsp. water

salt, to taste

1 tsp. white pepper

dash of sugar

Broth ingredients

2 parsley roots

1 onion

3 carrots

2 celery stalks

salt, pepper and sugar, to taste

☛ approx. 15 quart pot

Oifen ganif brendt dos hittle.
You can read the guilt on the thief's face.

Directions

Prepare chicken with kalochlach ingredients and form into balls about 1" in diameter. Set aside. Fill pot halfway with water, add ingredients and boil to make broth. Lower flame but keep broth boiling. Drop kalochlach into boiling broth, cover and continue to boil over a low flame for about 1 hour or until tender. If necessary, cook for an additional 10 - 12 minutes. Remove from stove, drain, cool and refrigerate.

This dish is prepared much like gefilte fish and many people serve it as an alternative. Serve cold with challah.

During one of our many conversations, Marlene asked me if I had a recipe for chicken kalochlach. I didn't know what she meant but then one Thursday, which was our recipe testing day, Marlene dropped in and mentioned kalochlach to Stella. "Oh" replied Stella, "I know what you mean. That's the last recipe your mother had me record."

Stella explained that Ma used to make it often for herself because it was so easy to digest. She would eat it cold with a slice of bread.

Breaded Chicken Breast
serves 6 - 8

Ingredients
6 chicken breasts (boneless and skinned)
$1/2$ cup matzo meal, enough to cover chicken
salt and pepper, to taste
$1/4$ tsp. garlic powder
oil, enough to cover fry pan
$1/8$ tsp. paprika
3 eggs (optional)
☛ approx. 9" fry pan

Directions
Mix matzo meal with salt, pepper, garlic powder and paprika. Set aside.
Beat eggs (optional) and set aside. Wash chicken, dip in dry mixture and,
if using eggs, dip in egg mixture. When using eggs it is necessary to dip
the chicken breasts in the dry mixture as well as the egg mixture a second
time. Cover chicken on both sides and fry in hot oil over medium flame
until golden brown (about 3 - 4 minutes on each side). Remove from fry
pan and place on paper towel to absorb excess oil and cool.

Can be frozen. To reheat, defrost, place in Pyrex dish, cover and place in
hot oven for 10 - 15 minutes. Can be served with cherry sauce, sweet 'n'
sour sauce or duck sauce. Do not freeze with sauce.

Chinese Chicken Livers
serves 4

Ingredients
1 lb. chicken livers
12 oz. bottle garlic spare-rib sauce
2 Tbsp. corn starch
2 Tbsp. oil
$3/4$ cup water
1 onion (sliced)
1 packet sweetener or 1 tsp. sugar
$1/2$ lb. unhatched eggs (optional)
☛ approx. 9" fry pan

Directions
Dilute corn starch with $1/2$ cup water until it is thick, but not totally dissolved and then set aside. Sauté onion in $1/4$ cup water and oil over medium flame for about 3 - 5 minutes, or until golden brown. Rinse livers in cold water and then add to onions. Continue to sauté for an additional 3 - 5 minutes over medium flame. Livers should not be overdone. Stir occasionally, lower flame and add garlic spare-rib sauce (the flame should be just warm enough to warm the sauce). Add corn starch mixture, stir and remove as soon as the sauce has thickened. If you are using unhatched eggs, add them at the very end, just prior to serving. (Cooking time should be no more than 15 - 18 minutes).

Serve on bed of white rice.

Men darf alah meshuganeh arois schtelen, un unz alah arine schtelen.
We're acting like lunatics.

Chicken Meat Loaf
with Vegetables

serves 7 - 9

Ingredients

1 lb. minced chicken (breast only)
1 egg
1 onion
$\frac{1}{4}$ tsp. garlic
4 tsp. matzo meal
4 Tbsp. ketchup
1 tsp. soya sauce
3 Tbsp. garlic spare-rib sauce (strong)
3 cloves fresh garlic
4 oz. apricot or peach jam
4 oz. tomato juice
4 oz. sweet 'n' sour Cantonese sauce
2 potatoes (cubed)
2 carrots (sliced)
$\frac{1}{2}$ zucchini (cubed)
4 oz. liquid chicken soup
☞ approx. 9" x 12" Pyrex dish

Men vert meineh sonim meshugeh.

They're acting like idiots.

140

Directions

Prepare sauce by mixing ketchup, soya sauce, spare-rib sauce and garlic powder. Line Pyrex dish with half the sauce and add onion and cloves of garlic. Mix minced chicken, matzo meal, egg and balance of the sauce together. Use an oval slotted spoon and place 5 loaves (approximately 4" x 2" x 2") on top of sauce in the Pyrex dish. Top with jam, chicken stock, tomato juice and sweet 'n' sour Cantonese sauce.

Bake, uncovered, at 350° for 15 minutes .

Remove from oven. Add vegetables, cover and return to oven for 45 - 60 minutes. Keep basting until vegetables are done.

Can be frozen.

Note

When using a slotted spoon always rinse it in cold water prior to filling it with the chicken mixture. This prevents chicken loaves from sticking together when they are being placed in Pyrex dish.

Ma used to say, **"Men legt altz dink arine in dem - nor..."** *("This recipe contains everything but the kitchen sink.")*

Chicken Meatballs
makes 36

Ingredients
1 lb. minced chicken (white meat only)
1 lb. minced veal
2 tsp. fresh parsley (chopped)
$1/4$ tsp. garlic powder
1 Tbsp. brown sugar
$1/2$ cup ketchup
1 tsp. soya sauce
1 Tbsp. garlic sauce
2 eggs
$1/2$ cup matzo meal
☛ approx. 10 quart pot and 9" x 12" cookie sheet

Directions
Mix garlic powder, brown sugar, ketchup, soya sauce, garlic sauce, eggs and matzo meal to meat. Set aside.

For sauce and further preparation follow recipe for Sweet 'n' Sour Meatballs (page 32).

This recipe is lighter than Sweet 'n' Sour Meatballs.

Chicken Nuggets
makes 72

Ingredients
1 lb. breast of chicken (cubed, skinned, boneless)
1 cup breadcrumbs or matzo meal
1 tsp. garlic powder
1 tsp. salt
pepper, to taste
2 eggs (beaten)

Directions
Mix breadcrumbs with garlic powder, salt and pepper. Wash chicken and dip into beaten egg, then into breadcrumb mixture. Repeat egg, breadcrumb dip (two times total) and then place on cookie sheet.

Bake at 350° for 45 minutes.

Serve with pineapple, Cantonese or cherry sauce on rice, or as is.

Der mentch tracht un Got lacht.
The best laid plans...

Chicken Wings
makes 16

Ingredients
2 lbs. chicken wings
1 1/2 tsp. garlic powder
1/4 cup oil
2 tsp. flour
3 cloves garlic (each one divided in half)
12 oz. bottle honey garlic spare-rib sauce
or
12 oz. bottle strong garlic sauce
☛ 2 approx. 15 quart pots

Directions
Wash and clean chicken wings in boiling water and sprinkle with garlic powder. Brown in hot oil on both sides for approximately 5 minutes. Remove wings from fry pan and discard the oil. Place wings on paper towel and set aside. Pour honey garlic sauce into clean pot. Bring sauce to a boil and lower the flame. Add the flour and mix thoroughly. Add browned chicken wings to the mixture and continue to boil for 20 - 25 minutes. Lower flame once again and continue to cook until sauce thickens, stirring constantly. Check to make sure that the wings are soft and that the sauce has thickened. If the wings are not soft, cook for an additional 5 minutes. Baste 2 or 3 more times.

Can be frozen. To reheat, defrost and place in covered Pyrex dish . Place in oven on medium heat for 15 minutes, or until hot.

Delicious with white rice.

Er iz frish un gezunt un meshugah.
He is hale and hearty and crazy.

Pineapple Chicken
serves 5

Ingredients
1 chicken (cut into eighths)
garlic powder, to taste
1/8 tsp. paprika
1 cup water
1/4 tsp. salt
1 cup sugar
3 Tbsp. corn starch
3 Tbsp. ketchup
3 Tbsp. oil
3/4 cup vinegar
10 oz. can pineapple tidbits (drained)
1 green pepper (cut into small pieces)
1/2 lb. mushrooms (cut into small pieces)
☛ 2 approx. 9" x 12" Pyrex dishes and 1 medium-size sauce pan

Directions
Preheat oven to 350°.

Clean chicken with boiling water and then season with garlic powder and paprika. Cover and bake for 1 hour.

To prepare sauce, heat water, salt, sugar, corn starch, ketchup, oil and vinegar over low flame. When mixture becomes thick and clear, add pineapple tidbits, green pepper and mushrooms. Let it simmer for a few minutes, remove from stove and set aside. When the chicken is done, remove from original pan (to remove fat) and transfer to a clean one. Pour sauce over chicken.

Bake, uncovered, for 40 - 50 minutes and baste occasionally.

Can be frozen with sauce. To reheat, defrost and place in pan. Cover and heat in medium to hot oven for about 15 minutes, or until hot.

Roast Turkey
serves 12 - 15

Turkey ingredients
8 - 10 lb. turkey (the larger, the juicier)
garlic powder, enough to cover turkey
2 - 3 bottles sweet 'n' sour pineapple sauce (36 oz. total)
ketchup, enough to cover turkey
1 large onion (sliced, optional)
1 tsp. oil (optional)

Stuffing
see Matzo Farfel (page 73)

☛ large roasting pan

Directions
Prepare stuffing and set aside. Cover baking pan with oil and sliced onion. Clean turkey with boiling water and set aside. Mix garlic powder, ketchup and pineapple sauce together and then spread this mixture all over the turkey. Place stuffing into the turkey just prior to putting it in the oven. Do not forget to sew the opening after inserting the stuffing.

Cover and bake at 350° for 1½ - 2 hours. Baste every 15 - 20 minutes. (Uncover after 1 hour and continue to cook for another hour or until soft and juicy). Keep basting. If the turkey is not soft after 2 hours, continue cooking for another 30 minutes. Keep basting every 10 minutes.

Remove turkey from gravy. Cool, skim and discard fat and allow to cool again. Skim and discard fat again. Reheat prior to serving.

Can be frozen. To reheat, defrost, cover and place in the oven on medium heat for 30 minutes or until hot.

Cooking instructions are the same with or without stuffing.

Southern Fried Chicken

makes 8 pieces

Ingredients

1 boiled chicken from soup (cut into eighths)
1 cup matzo meal
2 eggs
½ Tbsp. garlic powder
salt and pepper, to taste
¼ tsp. paprika
oil, enough to cover fry pan (approx. ¼ cup)
☞ round fry pan and approx. 9" x 12" Pyrex dish

Directions

Beat eggs and salt. Set aside. Mix garlic powder, matzo meal, paprika, salt and pepper together. Set aside.

Dip chicken pieces one by one first in egg and then in matzo meal mixture. Repeat dipping in egg and then dry mixture (two times total).

Fry chicken in hot oil turning chicken pieces once to brown on both sides (2 minutes each). Remove when browned and place on paper towel.

Can be frozen.

For years, my kids thought that I didn't know the difference between Southern fried chicken and boiled chicken. I had never done the egg-matzo meal dip twice, as stressed in this recipe. Needless to say, the breading always ended up in the pan and my children never believed that this recipe called for boiled, rather than raw, chicken. They were sure I was trying to salvage leftover boiled chicken. Only when this book was being compiled, did I realize that their doubts were justified. To redeem myself I explained what had happened. What a relief!

Beef Brisket

Hamburgers

Meat Loaf

Liver Knishes

Pepper Steak

Stewed Calf's Liver

Tongue

Tongue Sauce

Sweetbreads

Veal Chops

Veal Roast

Veal Spare-ribs

Shabbat

Holiday Treats

Light Lunches
and Pastas

Salads, Sauces
and Soups

Vegetables

Fish

Poultry

Meats

Desserts

Odds 'n' Ends

149

Beef Brisket
serves 10 - 12

Basic recipe
Ingredients
4 lbs. shell brisket (end cut)
2 Tbsp. chicken stock (dry)
2 Tbsp. garlic powder
2 Tbsp. dry mustard
$1/2$ cup ketchup
12 oz. bottle garlic spare-rib sauce

Directions
Mix chicken stock, garlic powder and mustard together and season brisket by rubbing ingredients onto meat. Make sure there is enough to lightly season the brisket on all sides (you may have to add a little of each). Add ketchup and spare-rib sauce.

Cover and bake at 350° for 2 - $2^1/2$ hour.

Turn brisket over onto the other side after $1^1/2$ hours. With a fork, check to see if meat is tender. If it is, remove from pan and cool. Slice brisket when it is cold.

Brisket is the type of meat that is easy to make for a crowd. It can also be frozen, but remember to always slice brisket prior to freezing. To reheat, defrost and add a drop of water and a drop of ketchup. Reheat on top of the stove over low to medium flame, covered for 10 - 12 minutes, or until piping hot.

A hartz feelt a beesem keshenah.
Loving minds think kindly of each other simultaneously.

Alternative method #1
Ingredients
Use ingredients as for the "basic recipe"

Directions
Cover the brisket with the dry ingredients only. Wrap very tightly in heavy aluminum foil wrap.

Bake in the oven at 350° for 1^1/$_2$ - 2 hours.

When the dry ingredients are baked, they form the gravy. Remove from the oven and cool. Slice into very thin slices when the brisket is cold.

Delicious!

Alternative Method #2
Ingredients
4 lbs. shell brisket (end cut)
1^1/$_2$ oz. package dry onion soup mix

Directions
Cover the brisket with the dry onion soup mix only. Wrap the brisket in heavy aluminum foil wrap.

Wrap very tightly and bake in the oven at 350° for 2 - 2^1/$_2$ hours.

This method produces a very delicious brisket as well. It is spicier than the other recipes. When done, remove from the oven and cool. Slice into very thin slices when brisket is cold. The soup mix creates the gravy.

Tsum schlimazel darf men oykhet hoben mazel.
Even for bad luck, you need good luck.

Hamburgers
makes 10

Ingredients
1$^1/_2$ lbs. minced steak
1 egg
3 Tbsp. oatmeal
1 onion (sliced)
oil, enough to cover fry pan
garlic powder, to taste
salt and pepper, to taste
☛ approx. 9" round fry pan

Directions
Mix meat, egg, oatmeal, garlic, salt and pepper together. Heat oil in fry pan and sauté onion. Place onion at the periphery of the fry pan and fry the burgers on both sides until brown.

Can be frozen. To reheat, defrost and wrap in aluminum foil. Place in hot oven for about 10 - 15 minutes.

Ayner veynt az di zuppe iz bitter, ayner veynt az di perel zeinen shiter.
One cries that life is a bitter brew and one cries that her pearls are too few.

Meat Loaf

makes 4 loaves

Ingredients

2 lbs. minced steak

or

1 lb. minced steak + 1 lb. minced veal

2 - 3 eggs

1 package dry onion soup

2 Tbsp. ketchup

2 tsp. dry mustard

garlic powder, to taste (approx. $1/8$ tsp.)

pepper

1 slice bread or chalah (soaked in water)

2 onions (sliced)

2 Tbsp. oil

$1/4$ tsp. paprika

☞ fry pan for use on the stove and in the oven

Directions

Mix meat, eggs, onion soup, ketchup, mustard, garlic powder, pepper and soaked bread in a large bowl. Consistency should be easy to work with. Cover fry pan with oil and sliced onions. Use wet oval slotted spoon to make 4 oval shaped loaves (4" x 2" x 2") and then place into the fry pan. Rinse spoon with cold water between forming each loaf. Top with paprika and brown over low flame for 30 minutes. Turn and top with oil/onion mixture and an additional drop of water, ketchup and paprika.

Bake at 350° for 30 minutes until brown. Baste occasionally.

Can be frozen.

Liver Knishes
(Jewish version of shepherd's pie)
makes 4 dozen

Filling ingredients
1 lb. uncooked chicken livers
2 Tbsp. water
4 onions
$^1/_2$ cup oil
salt and pepper, to taste
1 egg
1 whole chicken (skinned, boneless, cubed and boiled)

Dough ingredients
6 potatoes (boiled and mashed)
3 Tbsp. flour
salt and pepper, to taste
2 Tbsp. oil
☛ approx. 9" x 12" Pyrex dish

Yenem's tsouris ken icht farnemen.
Someone else's problems are easy for me to handle.

Filling directions

Stew onions in oil and water until soft and golden brown (about
10 minutes). Rinse chicken livers in cold water and add to mixture.
Continue to stew for an additional 20 minutes or until done. Add chicken
cubes and continue to cook for an additional 5 minutes. Set aside. Cool
and grind on fine cycle of the meat grinder. Add the egg to the mixture.
Add salt and pepper to taste and mix. Set aside.

Dough directions

Boil and mash potatoes. Add flour, salt, pepper and oil. Form a ball of
2 Tbsp. of filling and cover ball with dough approximately 3" in diameter.
Place onto lightly greased Pyrex dish.

Bake at 350° for 20 - 25 minutes.

Can be frozen prior to baking. To reheat, bake at 400° for 25 minutes on a
lightly greased cookie sheet. Do not defrost.

*If served as a main course, serve 2 - 3 knishes per person with corn
niblets and green peas. If served as a side dish, 1 per person is sufficient.*

My favourite!

Pepper Steak

serves 8 - 10

Ingredients

2 tsp. garlic powder
2 lbs. shoulder steak (cut into strips $1/2$" x 3")
1 Tbsp. corn starch
$1/4$ cup oil
2 cloves fresh garlic
2 Tbsp. soya sauce
1 cup water
3 celery stalks
1 onion
1 green pepper *
$1/2$ lb. mushrooms
2 potatoes
3 carrots
1 packet sugar substitute or 1 Tbsp. sugar
cauliflower, zucchini, yellow and/or red peppers or tomatoes (optional)

Directions

Wash and cube vegetables and set aside. Dilute corn starch with $3/4$ cup of cold water and set aside. Sauté onion in water and oil for 3 - 5 minutes and add strips of shoulder steak that have been seasoned in garlic powder. Brown meat in the oil. Chop fresh garlic into the meat. Add soya sauce and $1/4$ cup of water. Cook for 30 minutes or until meat is tender. Stir mixture and keep adding additional water if necessary (just a little). Then add the vegetables to the meat. Slowly, add mixture of cold water and corn starch to meat and vegetables. Keep stirring. Taste sauce and if it's too bitter (from the green pepper) add a touch of sugar and sweetener.

Can be frozen without the potatoes. They have a tendency to become soggy when frozen.

* When using green pepper, sweetener is usually required because green pepper can add a bitter taste.

Stewed Calf's Liver

Ingredients
3 slices calf's liver *
1 onion
2 Tbsp. oil
¼ cup water
1 cup garlic sauce (optional)
1 packet sweetener or dash of sugar (optional)
☞ approx. 9" round fry pan

Directions
Rinse liver in cold water. Sauté onion, oil and water, lightly for
3 minutes. Add garlic sauce and liver. Stew on a low flame for
10 minutes, until pink. If you prefer liver to be more well done, stew for
an extra 2 - 3 minutes.

Cannot be frozen. Always make it fresh.

Note
Liver should never be overcooked as it becomes tough and inedible.
It also has a tendency to be bitter but a bit of sweetener will help.

* Calf's liver is much softer than beef liver, so Ma used it
whenever possible.

Vos vet zayne, vet zayne.
What will be, will be.

Tongue

serves 6 - 8

Ingredients
1 medium-size calf's tongue *
☞ approx. 20 quart pot

Directions
Cover the tongue with water and boil over medium flame for about
1$^{1}/_{2}$ - 2 hours. Remove when tender. Peel tongue when hot (it is easier
to remove skin then). Cool and slice.

Can be served hot or cold.

* Calf's tongue tends to be softer than beef tongue and it is smaller in
size. Therefore, it needs less cooking time.

Fun honig loift men nit avec.
One doesn't run from a life as sweet as honey.

Tongue Sauce

Ingredients
19 oz. can tomato juice
5 packets sweetener or $1/3$ cup white sugar
1 cup brown sugar
4 Tbsp. garlic sauce
4 Tbsp. sherry (red wine or vermouth)
1 - $1^1/2$ cups golden raisins
$1/3$ cup lemon juice
☛ approx. 8 quart pot

Directions
Mix all of the above ingredients together and heat over low to medium flame for about 10 minutes. Cover and keep stirring occasionally. Taste until you are pleased with the taste. Remember the raisins tend to release a sweet taste as they are being cooked.

If serving the tongue in sauce, serve hot. Prepare sauce separately. When the tongue is sliced, place it in sauce. Heat and serve. For a tangier taste, let the tongue marinate in sauce for about 2 hours prior to heating. To heat tongue and sauce, cover and place in the oven at 350° until hot.

Sweetbreads

(thymus)
serves 6 as appetizer; 3 as main course

Ingredients
$1/2$ lb. sweetbreads (cut into small cubes) *
4 small carrots (cut into small pieces)
4 stalks celery (cut into small pieces)
$1/8$ tsp. garlic powder
salt and pepper, to taste
4 cloves garlic
1 onion
$1/4$ cup oil
2 cups water
potato (optional)
☛ approx. 10 quart pot

Directions
Season sweetbreads with garlic powder. Stew in oil, onion, garlic and $1/2$ cup of water, uncovered on a medium flame for 30 minutes. Add salt and pepper, to taste. Add vegetables and additional water. Cover and continue to cook, while still simmering on a low flame, for an additional 30 minutes. Water will keep stew moist. If potato is added the stew will be thicker.

Alternate method
Stew the sweetbreads in oil, onions, water and garlic cloves for about 45 minutes. Prior to stewing I suggest steaming sweetbreads in a double boiler for about 10 - 15 minutes, to ensure tenderness. Stew other vegetables separately for about 15 minutes. Add salt, pepper and garlic and then combine with vegetables. Cook over medium-low flame for another 20 - 25 minutes (covered) or until tender. Total cooking time is about $1 1/2$ hours.

* Thymus is softer than pancreas.

Veal Chops

serves 6

Ingredients
6 first-cut veal chops
oil, enough to cover fry pan
2 eggs (beaten with a drop of salt)
2 Tbsp. dry chicken soup mix
3/4 cup matzo meal
1 tsp. garlic powder
☞ approx. 9" x 12" Pyrex dish and 9" round fry pan

Directions
Wash and place veal chops on a board. Season with garlic powder and dry chicken soup mix. Coat with beaten eggs and then with matzo meal. Repeat egg dip and then matzo meal dip.

Fry in hot oil for a few minutes. Turn chops over and fry on other side. Remove chops from pan and place on paper towel to remove excess oil. Transfer to Pyrex dish, cover and bake at 350° for about 30 minutes. Lower heat, uncover and cook for an additional 10 minutes.

Can be frozen. To reheat, defrost and place in Pyrex dish with a drop of water or liquid chicken stock. Cover and bake on medium heat for about 15 minutes or until hot.

Vos tsu feel iz iberik.

Excess is superfluous.

Veal Roast
serves 12 - 14

Ingredients
6 lb. veal brisket (without pocket)
2 large onions (sliced)
1/2 bottle garlic sauce (strong)
1/2 cup ketchup
1 Tbsp. brown sugar
2 cloves fresh crushed garlic or 1 Tbsp. garlic powder *
☞ large roasting pan

Directions
Mix garlic sauce, ketchup, brown sugar and garlic. Season brisket with this mixture. Place sliced onions in roasting pan and then place seasoned brisket on top of the onions.

Cover and bake at 350° for 2 - 2 1/2 hours.

Use a fork to make sure the brisket is tender. Remove from oven, cool and slice.

* Fresh garlic is always preferable.

Excellent. Clara's favourite!

Klener dem oilem, gresser di simcha.
The smaller the crowd, the more joyful the party.

Veal Spare-Ribs
serves 4 - 6

Ingredients
1 lb. veal short ribs with bones (or baby veal ribs)
2 tsp. garlic powder
1/2 cup flour
1 tsp. dry mustard
1 tsp. salt
1 bottle garlic sauce (strong)
salt and pepper, to taste
☛ approx. 15 quart pot

Directions
Fill pot with water halfway and bring to a boil. Place ribs with salt in the boiling water and allow to cook for 10 - 15 minutes in order for ribs to soften. Remove and discard water. Set ribs aside.

Prepare mixture of flour, garlic powder, dry mustard, salt and pepper. Roll ribs in mixture.

Bring the garlic sauce to a boil over medium flame for about 5 minutes and allow to thicken slightly. Add seasoned spare-ribs to the garlic sauce. Leave uncovered and continue to boil for an additional 10 - 15 minutes. Continue to stir mixture. Make sure that the ribs are tender or continue to cook over low flame for an additional 5 - 7 minutes.

Serve on a bed of white rice.

Elaine's favourite!

Apple Cake

Apple Sauce

Blueberry Pie

Cheesecake

Hot Cheesecake with Lattice Topping

Chocolate Cake

Chocolate Whipped Cream Filling and Frosting

Chocolate Marshmallow Roll

Apple Strudel

Coffee Cake

Cream Cheese Dough

Gelatin Mold

Kichel

Lemon Pie Filling

Lemon Meringue Pie

Lemon Roll Cake

Marble Cake

Mandelbroit

Mocha Pie Filling

Onion Kichel

Orange Sherbet Mousse

Peach Compote

Turkish Delight Cookies

Shabbat

Holiday Treats

Light Lunches
and Pastas

Salads, Sauces
and Soups

Vegetables

Fish

Poultry

Meats

Desserts

Odds 'n' Ends

Apple Cake
serves 9 - 12

Ingredients
6 apples *
2 eggs
1 cup sugar
juice from 1/2 fresh lemon
1 tsp. cinnamon
1/2 cup oil
1 tsp. vanilla
3/4 cup flour (sifted)
1 tsp. baking powder
raisins (optional)
red maraschino cherries (optional)
☛ approx. 8" x 8" Pyrex dish

Directions
Preheat over to 375°.

Prepare batter and set aside. Mix eggs with sugar. Add oil, vanilla, flour, baking powder and set aside. Wash, peel and cut up apples. Sprinkle with lemon juice immediately, to avoid apples from turning brown. Place apples in Pyrex dish and sprinkle with cinnamon. If using raisins and/or cherries, sprinkle in with apples.

Pour batter over apples and bake for 45 minutes. Cool and cut into 2" squares. Can be frozen. Recipe can be doubled.

* You can also use peaches (6) or blueberries (1 large box of fresh blueberries, or enough to cover the bottom of the pan) but only when fruit is in season. If using blueberries, use sugar instead of cinnamon.

Excellent and easy to prepare. This cake has been made almost once a month for the past 10 years. We call it a "No Miss – Sure Success" cake.

Apple Sauce

serves 15 -18

Ingredients

12 MacIntosh apples
6 packets sweetener or $\frac{1}{4}$ cup sugar *
2 Tbsp. dry red gelatin (optional) **
☛ approx. 20 quart pot

Directions

Wash, peel and slice apples. Place them in large pot and fill the pot with enough cold water to cover the apples. Bring to a boil, adding sugar or sugar substitute to taste along with the gelatin. Cover, lower flame and let simmer for about 20 minutes. Taste intermittently. The average time for simmering is about 20 minutes, however, the longer the apples are cooked the softer the consistency. The end result should look like a compote with chunks of apples. If thicker apple sauce is desired - uncover and allow to simmer for an additional 10 minutes.

* When adding sugar or sugar substitute, it is necessary for you to adjust to taste.

** Ma liked food to look appetizing so she added gelatin for colour. Use the gelatin sparingly, otherwise the apple sauce will taste more like gelatin and have a much thicker consistency.

Josie's favourite!

Ma made apple sauce with sugar for some members of the family and with sweetener for others. If not for the jars being labeled accordingly, you could barely taste the difference.

Besser ain friendt eyder tsen soynem.
It's better to have one friend then to have ten enemies.

Blueberry Pie
serves 18

Filling ingredients
3 cups fresh blueberries in season
3 Tbsp. gelatin powder
$^1/_2$ cup sugar (optional)
1 tsp. corn starch

Dough
see dough for Haman Taschen (page 66)

☞ approx. 9" x 12" Pyrex dish

Directions
Prepare dough first and divide in half. Place dough into refrigerator and prepare filling.

Wash blueberries very well and carefully remove isolated stems and moldy berries. Add sugar, if necessary, corn starch and gelatin powder. Set aside.

Preheat oven to 350°.

Remove dough from refrigerator. Use half for the top of the pie and half for the bottom. Place dough on the bottom of the Pyrex dish and work as much of it up on the sides of the dish as possible (about $^1/_2$ way up). Pour the blueberry mixture onto the dough and cover with the second half of the dough. Mark dough superficially into squares 2" x 2" before baking. Sprinkle with sugar.

Bake for 30 minutes or until golden brown.

Joel's and Howard's favourite!

During Joel's four year program at Brown University in Providence, Rhode Island he took part in a six month exchange program at University College in London, England. When our friends, the Crolls, told us they were going to London and would be seeing Joel I thought of sending him a letter.

When I mentioned this to my mother, her first question was, "Can I bake a blueberry pie for Joel and would they mind taking it along?".

Naturally, the Crolls are special people and not only did they act as couriers par excellence, they made certain to bring back a photo as proof that it was delivered safely and devoured with gusto!

Thanks, Crolls!

Joel enjoying his blueberry pie

Cheesecake
serves 12 - 14

Base ingredients
$3/4$ box crushed graham wafers (12 ozs.)
$1/2$ cup brown sugar
$1/4$ lb. melted butter

Filling ingredients
$1 1/2$ lb. dry cottage cheese *
2 tsp. vanilla
1 cup white sugar
pinch of salt
1 cup milk
4 eggs (separated)

Choice of toppings
19 oz. can cherry pie filling
16 ozs. frozen raspberries (defrosted and drained)
19 oz. can pineapple pie filling
19 oz. can blueberry pie filling
$1/2$ - 1 lb. fresh strawberries, raspberries or blueberries in season.

☛ approx. 12" spring form pan

Eynems mazel iz dem anderins schlimazel.
One's good fortune is another's misfortune.

Base directions

Mix ingredients for base together. Remove 3 Tbsp. of base and set aside for topping. Place reserve in refrigerator and the balance into the spring form pan and pat it down. Line the sides of the pan as well.

Filling directions

Cream cheese with egg yolks and sugar. Mix in milk, salt and vanilla. Beat egg whites and fold into cheese mixture very gently. Pour mixture over the base and sprinkle with reserve from base.

Bake for 1 hour at 350°.

Cool with oven door open for 1 hour. Cover with desired topping.

Can be frozen prior to putting on the desired topping. To serve, defrost cake and add topping. Remember to remove the rim of the spring form pan prior to serving. Cake can remain on the bottom part of the pan.

* For richer tasting cake use cream cheese instead of cottage cheese.

This cheesecake recipe has been in our family for the last 15 years. It's always excellent!

Kleyne kinder, kleyne tsouris. Groyse kinder, groyse tsouris.
Little children, little problems. Big children, big problems.

Hot Cheesecake
with Lattice Topping
serves 12 - 14

Dough ingredients
1/2 lb. butter
1 cup sugar
2 eggs
4 Tbsp. sour cream
3 cups flour (sifted)
3 tsp. baking powder
pinch of salt
2 tsp. vanilla

Filling ingredients
1 lb. cottage cheese
2 eggs
1/4 cup sugar
2 tsp. sour cream
juice from 1 small lemon

☞ approx. 9" x 15" Pyrex dish

Az er iz mir a friendt, vel er a noyeh hoben ...
az er iz mir a soyneh, vel er platzen.

If he is my friend, he'll be happy for me ...
if he is my enemy and he's jealous, then he'll suffer with envy.

Dough directions

Mix dough ingredients together. Remove $^{1}/4$ of dough and set aside in the refrigerator for the top of the cheesecake. Wet your hands and pat the balance of the dough into the Pyrex dish. Try to push the dough along the sides of the dish.

Filling directions

Preheat oven to 350°.

Mix ingredients for filling together - except for the lemon juice – and pour over dough. Squirt filling with the lemon juice (you may not need all the juice – add to taste). Remove reserve dough from the refrigerator and divide into 10 rolls. Criss-cross over the topping. To form crisscross pattern - work on the diagonal - first in the width and then in the length.

Bake for 30 minutes.

Serve hot. Can be frozen.

Nice to serve with sour cream, yogurt, crushed pineapple, raspberry jam or defrosted and drained frozen raspberries.

Chocolate Cake
serves 12 - 15

Ingredients
4 eggs
$1/4$ lb. butter
2 squares dark chocolate
2 cups brown sugar
1 cup sour milk or $1/2$ cup sour cream + $1/2$ cup milk
2 tsp. baking powder
2 cups flour
☛ approx. 9" x 12" Pyrex dish, lined with waxed paper.

Directions
Preheat oven to 350°.

Cream butter and sugar. Melt chocolate and add to butter and sugar.
Cream again. Add eggs and sour milk or sour cream/milk mixture
alternately (i.e. 1st egg, $1/4$ of sour milk mixture, 2nd egg, $1/4$ of sour milk
mixture, etc.). Sift flour and baking powder. Blend into batter (on low
speed) and then pour into lined Pyrex dish.

Bake for 1 hour.

Remove from oven and turn onto cloth towel. Remove waxed paper and
allow to cool before turning over onto serving platter.

To frost (see next page), divide the cake in half horizontally.
Frost the bottom half, place second half on top and frost the entire cake.
Place in refrigerator.

Chocolate Whipped Cream Filling and Frosting

Ingredients

¹/₂ pt. whipping cream
¹/₂ cup icing sugar
¹/₄ cup cocoa
pinch of salt

Directions

Beat ingredients in order that they are listed until mixture is stiff and stands in peaks. Frost cooled cake and refrigerate.

Ma loved birthdays – her own as well as everyone else's.
A beautiful card was always included with the cake and the gift.

Chocolate Marshmallow Roll

(candy)
makes 4 rolls (80 pieces)

Ingredients
4 oz. unsweetened chocolate
1 Tbsp. butter
1 cup icing sugar (sifted)
1 egg
$1/2$ package white or coloured miniature marshmallows
$1/2$ cup finely chopped nuts (optional)
$1/2$ cup shredded coconut
☛ waxed paper and approx. medium-size saucepan

Directions
Melt chocolate over low flame. Add butter, icing sugar and egg. Stir until well blended. Place marshmallows and nuts into a large bowl. Pour hot mixture over the marshmallows a little at a time. Keep tossing lightly with a fork so that all marshmallows are coated.

Tear 4 strips of waxed paper and sprinkle with coconuts or chopped nuts if desired. Form mixture into 4 rolls on the waxed paper and roll in coconut until well covered. Roll (lengthwise) each roll tightly and freeze. Remove from freezer as needed. Cut into $1/2$" slices.

Self-praise is no recommendation but it's really delicious,
if I have to say so myself!

Apple Strudel
(similar to Viennese strudel)
serves 6 - 8

Ingredients
6 apples (MacIntosh or Cortland)
1/3 of a package puff dough or phyllo dough
2 Tbsp. dry red gelatin
raisins (optional)
red cherries (optional)
1/2 cup sugar
1 Tbsp. cinnamon
1 Tbsp. lemon juice
☞ approx. 9" x 12" cookie sheet

Directions
Roll dough out on floured board as thin as possible and set aside. Wash, peel and slice apples. Pour lemon juice over the apples to keep the apples from turning brown. Mix with cinnamon and sugar. Spread the apple mixture, cherries and raisins onto the dough. Sprinkle gelatin powder and roll into a log about 3" in diameter. Place on cookie sheet.

Bake at 350° for 30 - 40 minutes or until golden brown.

Allow to cool. Slice into 3" pieces on the diagonal and sprinkle with icing sugar before serving.

My father's and Ian's favourite dessert!

My cousin Phyllis faxed this recipe to me with this comment:
"Apple Strudel as I remember it from my Aunt Chana."

Coffee Cake

serves 10 - 12

Batter ingredients
1/4 lb. butter
1 cup sugar
2 eggs
1 cup sour cream
1 tsp. baking soda
1 1/2 cups flour
1 tsp. vanilla
1 1/2 tsp. baking powder

Filling ingredients
1/4 cup sugar
2 Tbsp. cinnamon
1/4 cup of raisins (optional)
1/4 cup of chopped walnuts (optional)

☛ approx. 9" x 9" Pyrex dish

Directions
Preheat oven to 350°.

Prepare filling and remove 3 Tbsp. for top of cake. Mix baking soda to sour cream and set aside. Cream butter and sugar and then add eggs. Add sour cream mixture to creamed butter, sugar and eggs. Add flour, baking powder and vanilla to creamed mixture. Grease pan with butter. Pour half of the batter into Pyrex dish and layer with the sugar-cinnamon-raisin-walnut mixture omitting the 3 Tbsp. that has been set aside. Pour remaining batter into the pan. Top with balance of filling.

Bake for 45 minutes.

Cool and cut into 2" square pieces. Easy to freeze and quick to defrost. Recipe can be doubled.

Cream Cheese Dough
(for pies and quiches)
makes 2 pie shells

Ingredients
1 cup butter
8 ozs. cream cheese
$1/2$ tsp. salt
2 cups flour
☞ approx. 9" round pie plate

Directions
Cream butter and cheese together. Add salt and flour. Continue to knead until blended.

Can be frozen.

A nar tor men nit vayzen kein halbeh arbeit.
Don't show a fool a job half-done.

Gelatin Mold
serves 12

Ingredients
2 boxes strawberry gelatin
2 boxes lime gelatin
14 oz. can peaches (drained)
14 oz. can bartlett pears (drained)
☛ approx. 12" x 15" round mold pan with hole in centre and
large glass serving plate.

Directions
Drain peaches and pears and set aside. Prepare the strawberry gelatin as directed on the box and use the juice from the fruit to make up the total amount of water as instructed on the package. Pour the strawberry gelatin into a large gelatin mold pan. Cool in the refrigerator for a few hours until almost ready. At that time arrange half of the fruit (center facing upwards) on top of the almost jelled gelatin. Allow to harden.

In a separate bowl prepare the lime gelatin in the same way as the strawberry gelatin. When almost ready pour over the strawberry gelatin. Add the balance of the fruit (center facing down). Refrigerate overnight.

When totally jelled, turn over onto a large glass serving plate just prior to serving. Place a hot cloth on top of the mold pan so that the gelatin comes out quickly prior to melting (you must work quickly). An alternative is to place the mold in hot water in the sink for a few seconds (no more than 10 seconds) and then turn over onto a large glass plate.
Refrigerate immediately.

Kichel
(plain)
makes 2 dozen

Ingredients
3 eggs
1^7/$_8$ cups flour (sifted)
^{1}/$_2$ tsp. of salt
oil for deep frying (approx. 2 cups)
☞ approx. 9" x 4" deep dish fry pan with basket

Directions
Roll out dough into a strip. Cut into 3" x 1" pieces. Make a knot or a twist. Deep fry in hot oil (test oil with a drop of dough or salt – if the oil sizzles, then it's hot enough) until golden brown (for approximately 3 - 4 minutes).

Drain on paper towel and sprinkle with icing sugar while hot.

Nor oif simchas!
May we meet only on happy occasions!

Lemon Pie Filling

for Lemon Meringue Pie (page 183) or Lemon Roll (see page184)

Ingredients
1 cup sugar
1 cup water
1 tsp. margarine or oil
3 Tbsp. corn starch
2 egg yolks
juice from 1 fresh lemon
pinch of salt
☛ medium-size saucepan

Directions
Mix corn starch and water. Add egg yolks, sugar and juice of the lemon.
Cook on a low flame until it thickens (approximately 5 - 10 minutes).
Keep stirring until it starts to bubble. Remove mixture from stove and
add margarine or oil. Let cool.

Note
To prepare this recipe for Passover, use 3 Tbsp. potato starch instead of
3 Tbsp. corn starch.

Arbeit macht dem leben zeese.
Being productive makes life worthwhile.

Lemon Meringue Pie
serves 8 - 10

Dough
see Cream Cheese Dough (page 179)

Meringue ingredients
2 egg whites
1/4 cup sugar

Filling
packaged lemon pie filling
or
Lemon Pie Filling (see page 182)

☞ approx. 9" Pyrex dish

Directions
Prepare packaged pie filling or Lemon Pie Filling. Set aside.

Roll out dough and place in Pyrex dish. Pierce sporadically with a fork.

Bake at 350° for 10 minutes.

Remove from oven, place filling on top of baked dough and set aside.

Meringue directions
Beat egg whites and sugar until stiff. Spoon meringue gently onto pie.

Bake at 400° for 8 - 10 minutes. The meringue should be golden brown.

Lemon Roll Cake
serves 12

Roll Ingredients
6 eggs
1 cup sugar
1 cup flour
1 tsp. baking powder
juice from $^1/_2$ lemon
icing sugar, enough to cover cookie sheet

Filling
packaged lemon pie filling
or
Lemon Pie Filling (page 182)
or
Mocha Pie Filling (page 189)
or
12 ozs. Raspberry Jam (page 196)

☛ approx. 10" x 12" cookie sheet, lined with waxed paper

Alles in aiynem iz nittau by keinem.
No one can have everything.

Directions

Mix flour and baking powder and set aside. Separate egg yolks from egg whites. Beat egg whites and add $1/2$ of the sugar to the egg whites. Set aside. Add the other $1/2$ of the sugar to the yolks. Combine the egg yolk and egg white mixture (beating on low speed). At the same time, add flour and baking powder mixture until smooth.

Pour onto cookie sheet and bake at 350° for 20 minutes. The batter should not rise.

While the batter is in the oven sprinkle icing sugar onto a dish towel. Remove cake from the oven, turn over onto the icing sugared surface and roll, lengthwise, while still hot (roll twice with the towel to achieve rounded effect). Put in lemon pie filling or your choice of mocha filling or raspberry jam. Place in refrigerator or directly into freezer.

To serve, remove from freezer approximately 3 hours before. Keep refrigerated.

Note

To prepare this recipe for Passover, use 1 cup Passover cake meal instead of 1 cup flour and 3 Tbsp. potato starch instead of 1 tsp. baking powder.

Ian's favourite!

A nar iz a nar.
A fool remains a fool.

Marble Cake
serves 12 - 15

Ingredients
12 eggs (at room temperature)
3 cups flour (sifted)
4 tsp. baking powder
1 Tbsp. whiskey, scotch or rye
3 Tbsp. cocoa with 4 Tbsp. warm water
2 cups sugar
3/4 cup oil
1/2 tsp. cream of tartar
☛ approx. 9" x 4" high round pan with hole in the middle

Directions
Preheat oven to 400°.

Mix cocoa and water and set aside. Sift flour and baking powder and set aside. Separate eggs, and beat egg whites with cream of tarter. Set aside.

Beat egg yolks with whisky, oil and sugar. Add sifted flour and baking powder mixture alternately with beaten egg whites. Mix with electric mixer for about 2 minutes. Pour into greased pan as follows: 1/3 batter, 1/2 cocoa mixture, 1/3 batter, 1/2 cocoa mixture, 1/3 batter. Mix gently around the hole with a spatula and then run a fork through the complete batter to get marble effect.

Bake at 400° for 10 minutes. Lower oven to 350° for 45 minutes. Test with toothpick for dryness to see if it's ready.

Place cake on a towel upside down and allow to cool for about 1 hour. Turn right side up and place on a serving tray. Before serving place a cloth lace doily on top of the cake and sprinkle with icing sugar to achieve a lacy effect. Remove the doily carefully.

This is a difficult recipe. It took me three tries to get it right!

Whenever I arrived home from a trip, there was always a welcome home cake - usually Ma's famous marble cake - and with it, the note below.

According to Josie, my mother would begin making arrangements for the cake three days before our return. Not only was she concerned about the pick up of the cake but also its presentation.

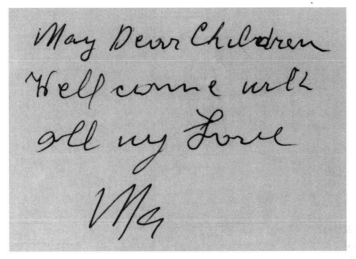

I always associated marble cake with birthdays and returning home from a trip. This was the note we always found attached to one of her "famous" marble cakes: "My dear children, welcome home. All my love, Ma."

My mother would make this cake on a moment's notice, on request. She would then say "It would be my pleasure, but I have one problem - no delivery service". There was always someone to pick up the cake or on occasion it was sent by taxi.

This cake is Jennifer's favourite and when asked to compare anyone's cooking to my mother's, Jennifer invariably made a face as if to say, "What a ridiculous question?" and would add, "Well no one can cook like my Bubby Chana!"

Mandelbroit

makes 4 dozen

Ingredients
2 eggs
$3/4$ cup sugar
$3/4$ cup oil
$2^1/2$ cups flour
1 tsp. baking powder
$1/2$ tsp. salt
$3/4$ cup nuts (optional)
☞ approx. 9" x 12" Teflon coated cookie sheet

Directions
Preheat oven to 350°.

Lightly grease cookie sheet and mix all ingredients together. Mix with a spatula and knead by hand until consistency is sticky. (If too wet add a drop of flour).

Divide mixture into 3 parts. Place lengthwise on a cookie sheet and shape into logs about $1^1/2$" x $3/4$".

Bake for 20 minutes until golden brown.

Remove from oven and slice on the diagonal (every $1/2$") and return to oven for an additional 5 - 7 minutes. Turn oven off and leave mandelbroit in for an additional 45 minutes so it will become dry and crispy.

Mandelbroit can be stored in a cookie tin for 2 - 3 weeks but it's usually eaten up long before!

Mocha Pie Filling
serves 12

Filling ingredients
1 pt. whipping cream
1 tsp. dry instant coffee
$1/2$ tsp. vanilla
1 Tbsp icing sugar
1 Tbsp. cocoa

Dough
see Lemon Roll (page 184)

Directions
Beat whipping cream and sugar gradually. Add coffee, cocoa and vanilla.
Follow directions for lemon roll (page 184), only fill with mocha filling.

A ma geyt mit a pa.
A mother always goes with a father.

Onion Kichel

makes 3 dozen

Ingredients

2 cups flour
2 tsp. baking powder
$1/2$ cup oil
2 eggs
3 large onions (finely grated)
3 Tbsp. sugar
2 tsp. salt
$1/4$ tsp. pepper
1 Tbsp. shortening
2 Tbsp. poppy seeds
☛ approx. 9" x 12" cookie sheet

Directions

Preheat oven to 350°.

Mix all ingredients together. Knead and roll out the dough on a floured surface until $1/4$" thick. Cut into half moon shapes and place on an oiled cookie sheet.

Bake at 350° for 10 - 12 minutes or until golden brown.

For a dryer kichel, bake for an additional 3 - 5 minutes. Turn oven off and leave the kichel in the oven with the door closed for another 5 minutes. These can last for about 10 days.

Marlene Briskin's father, Schmiel, loved these so much that a batch was sent to him in Jerusalem for his 90th birthday. These were also Uncle Meilach's favourite!

Orange Sherbet Mousse

Ingredients
2 boxes orange gelatin
1 pt. orange sherbet
1 box pineapple gelatin
1 pt. lemon sherbet (margarita)
1 small can crushed pineapple
1 can mandarin oranges
3 cups boiling water
cherries (optional)
chocolate shavings (optional)
☛ approx. 12" x 15" round pan with a hole in the center

Directions
Drain pineapple and mandarin oranges (keeping the liquid) and set aside. Prepare the gelatin as directed on the package but use the juice of the fruits instead of water (you may have to make up the difference in water). Melt in sherbet. Add pineapple and oranges. Stir. Refrigerate overnight in large gelatin mold pan.

Turn over onto large glass tray just prior to serving. This must be done quickly. Fill sink with hot water, dip gelatin mold into hot water for a split second and the gelatin should easily release from the pan. If not, put a hot towel around the pan for a minute or so and try again. Garnish with cherries and or chocolate shavings, or both. Refrigerate immediately.

Er ken tsu zammenfeeren a vant mit a vant.
He's a smooth talker.

Peach Compote
serves 12 - 15

Ingredients
1 basket of peaches in season
7 packets sweetener + $^3/_4$ cup sugar or 1 $^1/_2$ cups of sugar
1 Bartlett pear
☛ approx. 20 quart pot

Directions
Blanche peaches in boiling water and peel. Peel pear. Place peaches and pear in the pot and cover with water by about 1 - 2 inches. Add sugar substitute and sugar. Cover. Boil for about 8 - 10 minutes. Uncover and taste. Add more sugar or sugar substitute if necessary. Cook, uncovered, on medium flame for an additional 10 minutes. Let cool and then refrigerate.

Note
Can be made with sugar only, but sweetener only may leave a bitter aftertaste.

My favourite and Clara's favourite too!

Delicious!

Fur gezunt un kum gezunt.
Go in health and return in health.

Turkish Delight Cookies
makes 3 dozen

Dough ingredients
1/4 lb. butter
1/4 lb. cream cheese
1/2 cup flour

Filling
3 large squares Turkish delight (assorted colours)
or
1/4 lb. diced Turkish delight (assorted colours)

☞ approx. 9" x 12" cookie sheet

Directions
Preheat oven to 350°.

Cream butter and cheese and slowly add flour.   Place in refrigerator for 1 - 2 hours. Roll dough on floured board until smooth (about 1/8" thick). Cut into triangles. Insert small pieces (one or two) of Turkish delight at the widest end. Roll tightly from widest to narrowest side. Shape into half moons and place on cookie sheet.

Bake for 20 minutes or until golden brown.

Can be frozen.

Excellent!

Sholom aleichem, aleichem sholom.
Welcome home in peace.

Jam

Sour Milk

Sour Pickles

Sour Tomatoes

Happy Home Recipe

What You Won't Find in This Book

Shabbat

Holiday Treats

Light Lunches and Pastas

Salads, Sauces and Soups

Vegetables

Fish

Poultry

Meats

Desserts

Odds 'n' Ends

Jam
raspberry, blueberry, strawberry and peach *

Ingredients
your choice of berries in season **
sugar
☛ mason jars and approx. 20 quart pot

Directions
Sterilize jars and set aside with the opening of the jars faced down on paper towel so the jars won't get contaminated. Wash the berries very well. Measure 1 cup of berries to 1 cup of sugar. When combing berries and sugar, it is sometimes advantageous to allow the mixture to remain in the bowl for approximately 1 hour prior to boiling (this makes the jam a little thicker).   Bring the mixture to a boil and then let simmer for 40 minutes over medium to high flame. Stir occasionally during boiling period. You must watch the jam, so that it doesn't boil over. After 40 minutes, the mixture should be thick.

Pour hot jam into hot jars to the top leaving about $1/4$ of an inch of space. Seal tightly and turn jars upside down to create a vacuum. This increases the firmness of the seal and maintains sterility without using wax or any other sealant.

Cool and refrigerate.

* Raspberry, blueberry and strawberry jam are made the same way but for peach jam use 2 cups of peaches to 1 cup of sugar and at the end add 1 cup of sugar to the pot.

Can be refrigerated for about 6 weeks prior to opening. When the jam has been opened, it can only stay for 2 - 3 weeks.

** I find that berries are best in middle to late summer. I usually buy them by the case mainly because of the work involved in making jam. I prepare a number of jars of jam at one time and give them as gifts for Rosh Hashanah and Succoth.

When I asked my mother why she turns the finished filled jars of jam upside down, she answered ,"I do it, because my mother did it!". How's that for confidence and trust!

Sour Milk

Ingredients
3/4 glass whole milk
2 Tbsp. sour cream

Directions
Add sour cream to milk and let it stand at room temperature for an entire day. It should turn "bluish" as the cream rises to the top.

Like yogurt, sour milk can be eaten with cheese blintzes or other dairy dishes and should be eaten fresh.

I remember seeing a glass of milk sitting on the window sill and never knowing why. I don't recall ever tasting it either!

Er hot im opgeton oif terkish.
He double-crossed him.

Sour Pickles
(half-sours)

Ingredients
12 Kirby pickles (approx. 4" long) *
1/2 cup pickling spice
2 cloves of garlic
1/2 cup course pickling salt
6 cups cold water
3 celery stalks
2 roots pickling dill
☞ jars to hold 8 cups of water

Directions
Wash pickles and celery and arrange in a jar in an upright position along with half of the pickling spice, 2 cloves of garlic and half of the pickling dill. Set aside.

Mix 6 cups of cold water with 1/2 cup of the course salt. Place in a large bowl and stir until melted. Taste. Put water and salt mixture into the jar until the mixture covers the pickles. Add the balance of the pickling spice and the pickling dill. Let this stand on the counter at room temperature, uncovered, for one day. Check by tasting and if it is satisfactory, let it stand for an additional 2 days, uncovered. When the pickles turn greenish brown, cover and refrigerate.

Can last for about 3 weeks.

* For best results buy pickles in season at the end of the summer.

Sour Tomatoes
(half-sours)

The recipe for tomatoes is the same as the one for pickles with the following exceptions:

1
Substitute the pickles for 12 small green tomatoes. Tomatoes should be firm. * You can use either red tomatoes or rose tomatoes.

2
Tomatoes need more salt than pickles. Use $^3/_4$ cup pickling salt instead of $^1/_2$ cup.

3
Tomatoes take longer to sour. Leave them on the counter for 2 days, uncovered, then cover and leave on the counter or outside for another 2 - 3 weeks. Tomatoes are ready when they change colour from light green to dull olive green.

* For best results buy tomatoes in season at the end of the summer.

Az men lebt, derlebt men.
If we live long enough, anything can happen.

In September, 1993, our friend Normie Malus wanted to learn the technique of making sour pickles and tomatoes. He had never met my mother, but was familiar with her cooking prowess, by reputation. His theory was that if you are going to learn something, pick the best teacher possible.

He asked me if it would be convenient for him to spend a morning watching Ma do her thing. I, in turn, checked it out with Ma and although she wasn't delighted, she agreed. This was probably because Stella would be with her to keep everything under control.

Normie arrived, brought her a gift, watched her technique and left. He reported that he had a wonderful time and he hoped that one day he would be able to make the sours and deliver them to her. Unfortunately, the best laid plans...

My mother, on the other hand, told Stella that she didn't have such a wonderful time because she never liked to have a man around the kitchen. In addition, Normie's visit meant she had to get up early in order to have her hair done and get the apartment into "ship shape"! She ended up by saying, "Okay, let's forget about it, it's done and over with and that's that. I'm glad he had a good time!"

During the recipe testing, Stella filled me in on what Ma really said that day. Somehow, these were not the words I heard. Hence, I think it's worthy of printing the truth.

Ma confided in Stella that she couldn't understand why a busy notary would be interested in taking time off his schedule to make pickles and tomatoes. She had doubts about Normie, in general. The additional comments went something like this:
  - "My daughter and her bright ideas - always looking for projects for me."
  - "Why couldn't he send his wife?"
  - "Isn't it a woman's place to be in the home and in the kitchen?"

Then came the rationalization:
"Maybe I should open a cooking school to help my Evelyn and her friends. Actually, why am I complaining? I should be honoured! Anyway, maybe Evelyn's friend asked her for this favour and she wasn't able to refuse. Maybe she didn't want to hurt his feelings - I guess I shouldn't jump to conclusions - probably she had no choice!"

One of Ma's qualities was her ability to look at both sides of the coin and occasionally come to terms with a situation. Much like Teyve, she handled this situation as she handled others in her lifetime by saying, "On the other hand..." Yes, there always was another hand!

One of my paintings that I gave to my mother. On the back of the canvass I wrote,
"Dear Ma, may you constantly be surrounded by pots and flowers. Love Chava, 1981"

Happy Home Recipe

The last recipe is one that I found in our kitchen at *It-L-Do* in Trout Lake. It's rather easy to follow. The cost is minimal and the satisfaction is most gratifying. Basically it agrees with anyone and everyone who tries it.

Ingredients
4 cups of Love
5 Tbsp. of Hope
2 cups of Loyalty
2 Tbsp. of Tenderness
3 cups of Forgiveness
4 quarts of Faith
1 cup of Friendship
1 barrel of Laughter

Directions
Take loyalty and love. Mix thoroughly with faith. Blend tenderness, kindness and understanding. Add friendship and hope. Sprinkle with laughter. Bake it with sunshine. Serve generous helpings daily.

One of my mother's earliest sewing projects

What You Won't Find in This Book

Not all of my mother's recipes have been included in this book, because many of them were never written down. However, the real reason is really that they require too much detail, effort and patience in their preparations. Even Ma only prepared some of these dishes on very special occasions.

Blueberry *sponchkes* (doughnuts) were usually made at 5 a.m. at our country house in Trout Lake. My father loved sponchkes and after he died in 1964, Ma could never bring herself to make them again.

I remember eating *Teiglach* in our St. Urbain Street kitchen when I was a child. I guess they were too sticky to make regularly and I can't remember seeing them since I was about 10 years old.

Chopped herring was another dish of my youth. I haven't seen my mother's chopped herring in years and I can't even recall what it looks like or how it was handled by my palate.

Kishka and *Helzel* are two other dishes my mother never recorded. Even though she did not pass along these recipes, they still remind me of a humorous family anecdote involving the superstition not to show on yourself. This superstition cautions against describing someone else's malady by indicating it on your own body. Should you not take heed, the disease could become contagious. One Friday night at the dinner table, Joel - who had just started medical school - was talking about the various organs of the body. Naturally, the conversation turned to food. Ma recalled the days when she would make kishka (stuffed derma) and helzel (stuffed skin of the neck of the chicken). Of course, this was before people began to develop healthier eating habits. Since my kids had no idea of what kishka and helzel were, Ma began to describe the dish by placing her hands on her own neck. Joel couldn't resist and said: "Bubby, don't show on yourself". We all had a good laugh but never did get the recipe!

Notes

Metric conversion
(approximate equivalents)

1 quart	1 litre
1 pint	1/2 litre
1 cup	250 ml
3/4 cup	175 ml
2/3 cup	150 ml
1/2 cup	125 ml
1/3 cup	75 ml
1/4 cup	50 ml
1 tablespoon	15 m
1 teaspoon	5 ml
1/2 teaspoon	2 ml
1/4 teaspoon	1 ml
1/8 teaspoon	1/2 ml
2.2 pounds	1 kilogram
1.1 pound	500 grams
12 ounces	300 grams
8 ounces	250 grams
4 ounces	125 grams
2 ounces	62 grams

When cooking and baking remember these 3 things; any, or all, of which can alter the finished product:

1. Climatic conditions (e.g. humidity, temperature and atmospheric pressure)

2. Variations in oven conditions (distribution of heat) and type of oven used (i.e. gas or electric)

3. Experience of the chef – probably the most important factor

Metric baking temperatures

200°F	100°C
250°F	120°C
275°F	140°C
300°F	150°C
325°F	160°C
350°F	180°C
375°F	190°C
400°F	200°C
425°F	220°C
450°F	230°C
475°F	240°C
500°F	260°C

British Measure — Metric Measure

British Measure	Metric Measure
8" square pan x 2" deep	20 x 5 cm
9" square pan x 2" deep	22 x 5 cm
8" x 4" x 3" loaf pan	20 x 10 x 7 cm
9" x 5" x 3" loaf pan	22 x 12 x 7 cm
10" bundt pan x 4" deep	25 x 10 cm
8" round pan x 1$3/4$" deep	20 x 4 cm
7" x 11" oblong pan	30 x 20 x 5 cm
9" x 13" oblong pan	33 x 22 x 5 cm
9" pie plate	22 x 4 cm
10" x 15" cookie sheet	40 x 30 cm

Tribute Honouring the Late Annie Katz, of Blessed Memory

by Professor Michael Herschorn

A Lucky Move:
Mešanneh Māqôm, Mešanneh Mazzāl

Author's Note
Professor Michael Herschorn, a very dear friend of ours for many years, was one of my mother's "favourites". She always enjoyed talking with Michael about life and philosophy. For his part, Michael, as much a Talmudist as a mathematician, always took my mother's expressions just one step further. The following pages are his tribute to her. I am most grateful to him for having taken the time and effort to prepare this essay.

Michael and my mother in Trout Lake

A Lucky Move: משנה מקום, משנה מזל

Honouring the Memory of the Late Anna Katz: לז״נ חנה בת ר׳ יצחק ע״ה

Introduction

The late beloved Anna Katz [חנה בת ר׳ יצחק ע״ה] was proud of her Judaic heritage. Unlike most people of her generation and origins, she was well-versed in rabbinic Yiddish, and was delighted when she had the occasion to use it. Rabbinic Yiddish is rich in allusions to the Mishnaic, Talmudic, and Aggadic literatures, and its vocabulary has a higher Hebraic content than standard Yiddish. To use it properly and effectively, as she did, requires a measure of familiarity with the traditional sources.

One expression she used frequently was משנה מקום, משנה מזל [*mĕšanneh māqôm, mĕšanneh mazzāl*], a move will change your *mazzāl* (literally: changing location is changing *mazzāl*). We shall investigate the background and development of this locution.

Mazzāl: מזל

During the first half millennium of the current era there was some rabbinic opposition to the introduction of notions from astrology into religious belief, terminology, or practice. This opposition had only a limited success; the popular Jewish (and even rabbinic) *Weltanschauung* had begun to accommodate ideas which, in the generations from Ezra to Rabbi Judah Hanassi, would have been considered borderline, if not rank, heresies. Astrology taught that the relative positions of heavenly bodies determined the course of events on earth, and *mazzāl*, a Hebrew word originally meaning *planet* or *constellation*, became the carrier of astrological baggage into the Jewish world.

Talmudic sources

The rabbis held astronomy in high regard. Although this may have been motivated in part by the developing practical importance of astronomy in fixing the liturgical calendar, there seems to have been a "pure" component as well.[1]

אר״ש בן פזי א״ר יהושע בן לוי משום בר קפרא
כל היודע לחשב בתקופות ומזלות ואינו חושב
עליו הכתוב אומר ואת פועל ה׳ לא יביטו
ומעשה ידיו לא ראו. א״ר שמואל בר נחמני א״ר
יוחנן מנין שמצוה על האדם לחשב תקופות
ומזלות שנאמר ושמרתם ועשיתם כי היא
חכמתכם ובינתכם לעיני העמים. איזו חכמה

ובינה שהיא לעיני העמים הוי אומר זה חישוב
תקופות ומזלות.[2]

R. Simeon b. Pazzi said in the name of R. Joshua b. Levi on the authority of Bar Qappara: He who knows how to calculate the cycles and planetary courses, but does not, of him Scripture saith, *but they regard not the work of the Lord, neither have they considered the operation of his hands.*[3] R. Samuel b. Naḥmani said in R. Joḥanan's name: How do we know that it is one's duty to calculate the cycles and planetary courses? Because it is written, *for this is your wisdom and understanding in the sight of the peoples:*[4] what is wisdom and understanding in the sight of the peoples? Say, that is the science of cycles and planets.[5]

In the era of epicycles, when astronomy was naked-eye astrometry combined with more or less reasonable speculation, it was difficult, if not impossible, to delineate the boundary between astronomy and astrology. Since Judaism approved of astronomy, how could it keep astrology out?

The short answer is that it couldn't. Many earlier authorities are reported as denying that *mazzāl* can have any effect on Israel, but leaving open the possibility that it can determine the future for non-Israelites. Others went quite far

---

[1] English versions of quoted talmudic passages are based on the Soncino English Translation of the Babylonian Talmud.

[2] שבת ע״ה.

[3] Isa. V, 12

[4] Deut. IV, 6

[5] B. Shabbat 75a

in their acceptance of astrology, not seeming to be bothered by its limitation of Divine Providence and human free will.

איתמר רבי חנינא אומר מזל מחכים מזל
מעשיר ויש מזל לישראל. רבי יוחנן אמר אין
מזל לישראל.[6]

It was stated, R. Ḥanina said: The planetary influence gives wisdom, the planetary influence gives wealth, and Israel is under planetary influence. R. Joḥanan maintained: there is no *mazzāl* (planetary influence) on Israel.[7]

Medieval attitudes

The rabbinic imagination developed an allegorical personification of the planets and stars that made interesting and effective Midrash. Whether the rabbis involved were aware of the potential side-effects on the more literal-minded is not clear, but by the Saboraic period many of the rabbis accepted the factuality of their predecessors' flights of imagination. Once at this stage, the grounds for denying astrology any respectability become tenuous indeed.

By the XIIth century, the continued growth of these intellectual weeds was seen by Maimonides as a serious danger for Judaism, and he took upon himself the task of extirpating astrology, root and branch. This task was made difficult because the luxuriant growth of astrological concepts was rooted in talmudic discussions. Nevertheless, he minced no words, declaring that

it is the object and centre of the whole Law to abolish idolatry and utterly uproot it, and to overthrow the opinion that any of the stars could interfere for good or evil in human matters.[8]

In the *Letter to the Men of Marseilles* he categorized astrology as

a disease, not a science, a tree under the shadow of which all sorts of superstitions thrive, and which must be uprooted in order to give way to the tree of knowledge and the tree of life.[9]

But it is a rare physician who can do a thorough self-examination, and Maimonides, classical

Judaism's greatest philosophical thinker, was no exception. The Mishneh Torah, his *magnum opus* and a pioneering yet authoritative halakhic work, contains the following:

כל הכוכבים והגלגלים כולן בעלי נפש ודעה
והשכל הם. והם חיים ועומדים ומכירין את מי
שאמר והיה העולם. כל אחד ואחד לפי גדלו
ולפי מעלתו משבחים ומפארים ליוצרם כמו
המלאכים.[11]

The stars and the heavenly spheres are all beings possessed of souls, knowledge and intelligence. They are alive and rise to recognize the ineffable, by whose word the world came to exist. Each and every one, according to his stature and rank, praises and glorifies his creator in the manner of the angels.[12]

A century later, the Zohar could maintain that

הכל תלוי במזל ואפילו ספר תורה שבהיכל.[13]

Everything depends on *mazzāl*, even the holy Torah scroll maintained in the sanctuary of the Temple.[14]

As if to prove that a foolish consistency is the hobgoblin of small minds, this maxim is repeated with a qualification:

אין מזל לישראל ואע״ג דכלא תליא במזלא
אפילו ספר תורה שבהיכל.[15]

Mazzāl does not exist for Israel, this despite the fact that everything is determined by *mazzāl*, even the holy Torah scroll maintained in the sanctuary of the Temple.[16,17]

The immediate background

The part of the musaf services for Rosh Hashanah and Yom Kippur that receives the most popular attention is the section beginning with *Ûnetanneh*

---

[6] שבת קנו.

[7] B. Shabbat 156a

[8] Guide for the Perplexed, Part 3, Chap. XXXVII (Translation: M. Friedländer)

[9] Quoted as Steinschneider, Cat. Bodl. col. 1903 in the Jewish Encyclopedia, q.v., Astrology

[11] משנה תורה, מדע, הלכות יסודי התורה פ״ג ט׳

[12] Mishneh Torah, Foundations of the Torah, Chap. LVIII, 9

[13] זוהר במדבר קל״ד

[14] Zohar, Numbers 134

[15] תקוני זוהר ק״מ

[16] Tiqqunei Zohar, Chap. 140

[17] The Zohar and the Kabalists who followed in its footsteps built even more castles in the cosmos, and in the process added a new feature to astrology. Classical astrology is unidirectional: the cosmic influences cannot themselves be influenced, and one's destiny is written indelibly in the stars. The Kabalists effectively made it bidirectional by insisting that the mundane acts of humans changed the entire cosmos.

tōqeph. The *payyeṭān* (liturgical poet) describes the heavenly procedure for judging humans on Rosh Hashanah for their deeds of the year just completed. Their futures are inscribed in a celestial ledger which, to allow for updates made possible by repentance, is not sealed until Yom Kippur.

The worshipper is brought to a state of ever higher tension by the repetitive imagery, and can hardly wait for the release provided by the coda when the congregation responds in unison:

‫ותשובה ותפילה וצדקה מעבירין את רוע הגזרה!‬

Repentance, prayer and acts of charity [*or* righteousness] will avert the harshness of the decree!

The artistry is effective: it takes a hard heart indeed not to be swept up in the emotional undertow, and considerable perversity not to commit oneself to moral and religious self-improvement during the coming year.

The *payyeṭān* made selective use of homiletic material in the tractate Rosh Hashanah. The principal source for his coda is the sixth of a sequence of eight consecutive High Holyday "sermon outlines" by R. Isaac.

‫ואמ״ר יצחק ד' דברים מקרעין גזר דינו של אדם.‬
‫אלו הן: צדקה צעקה שינוי השם ושינוי‬
‫מעשה. ... וי״א אף שינוי מקום.‬18

R. Isaac further said: Four things cancel the doom[19] of a man, namely, charity, supplication, change of name, and change of conduct....[20] Some say that change of place [also avails].[21]

Our interest is in the scholium "Some say that change of place also avails", but a general comment on the quotation is in order. The reader should not suppose that the changes of name and place are Jonah-like attempts to "flee from the presence of the Lord"; viewed from an appropriate perspective, all the items are subcases of repentance. [22]

To summarize: an anonymous talmudic authority asserted that, under circumstances we have omitted, but in the context of repentance during the Days of Awe, doom can be averted by change of location.

A lucky way out

In talmudic usage the term *mazzāl* always bore an astral-related meaning. This appears to have remained the case through the period of Maimonides. At some later date, there was a semantic broadening to include the more abstract and operationally vacuous fate-destiny-luck axis within the semantic range of *mazzāl*. By replacing the astrological referents of *mazzāl*, such as they are, by the unspecific connotations of *fate* or *destiny*, one could paper over and ignore the bizarre cosmic elements behind the scenes.[23] Once the shift had become established, there was a fresh vocabulary available for the coinage of new phrases. The scholium to R. Isaac's "four things" can be given a particularly euphonious rewording as ‫משנה מזל‬ ‫,משנה מקום‬ [*mešanneh māqôm, mešanneh mazzāl*], and this is presumably the origin of the dictum.

The semantic shifting continued, and *mazzāl* came to be understood as (good) fortune.[24] *Mešanneh māqôm, mešanneh mazzāl* took on a new life, it being understood as advice to the unfortunate to try again in a different location.

Still not bad. Faith and begorra, 'tis the luck of the Jews![25]

---

18 ‫ראש השנה טז:‬

19 i.e., if done during the ten Days of Penitence avert the harshness of the divine decree.

20 The prooftexts are omitted.

21 B. Rosh Hashanah 16b

22 The classical talmudic commentators have little to say here, not even on the ineffectiveness of hiding out in Argentina under an assumed name. Suffice it to say that, with a proper contextual understanding, there are good (even "modern") grounds for accepting "changes of name and place". From that perspective,

R. Isaac's sermon outline was "right on", and could be used as the basis for an excellent High Holyday sermon in a twentieth century synagogue. Moreover, that understanding harmonizes the positions of R. Isaac, the authors of the scholium, and the *payyeṭān*. Since it is not central to our main concern, we move on. Hint for those interested: Vayyiqra Rabbah XXXII, 5, B. Giṭṭin 11b, B. Sanhedrin 17b, Abot I, 7, and generalize (and then generalize once again).

23 As a bonus, one can take these to be Divine Providence, thereby lessening the potential for heresy.

24 Yiddish *mazl* reflects this process and the shifts probably occurred in tandem. Although *mazl* retains the meaning of zodiacal sign in Yiddish, it is used principally to mean luck or good fortune. (Try "What's your *mazl*?" as a pickup line at a Yiddish singles bar; you might get *mazldik*!)

25 Thanks are due to Evelyn Gold, daughter of the late Anna Katz, for suggesting the topic *mešanneh māqôm, mešanneh mazzāl*.

Index